AF669266

Azure Bicep QuickStart Pro

From JSON and ARM Templates to Advanced Deployment Techniques, CI/CD Integration, and Environment Management

Selina Threxan

Published by: GitforGits

Publisher: Sonal Dhandre

www.gitforgits.com

support@gitforgits.com

Printed in India

First Printing: July 2024

ISBN: 978-81-974165-8-3

Cover Design by: Kitten Publishing

Prologue

I still remember the day I first encountered Azure Bicep. The sun was shining, and I was in the middle of a demanding project that called for the management and deployment of a plethora of Azure resources. Working with JSON-based ARM templates was becoming increasingly difficult, and I knew there had to be a better solution. That's when I came across Azure Bicep, a tool that would change the way I approached Azure deployments.

My experience with Azure Bicep started out of necessity. I was tasked with a high-stakes project for a client who required a robust, scalable, and secure Azure infrastructure on a very short timeline. I had heard of Bicep and decided to give it a try. The initial learning curve was steep, as I had to adapt from my familiar JSON habits to Bicep's declarative syntax. However, as I dug deeper, I realized that Bicep was more than just a tool; it represented a significant improvement in managing infrastructure as code.

One particularly difficult evening, I encountered a deployment issue that necessitated quick adaptation to changing client requirements. Traditional methods would have been slow and cumbersome, but Bicep's modular approach enabled me to divide the deployment into manageable chunks. I can vividly recall the moment when everything came together. I designed reusable modules, integrated them seamlessly, and deployed the infrastructure efficiently. The deployment was a success, and the client was ecstatic. This experience marked a turning point in my life. I realized that if Azure Bicep could transform my work, it could also help others facing similar challenges. That is why I chose to write "Azure Bicep QuickStart Pro." My goal is to share the insights, techniques, and strategies I've learned so that you can fully utilize Azure Bicep in your projects.

In this book, you will learn the fundamentals of JSON syntax and how to write ARM templates. Then we'll look at Bicep's declarative syntax and its powerful features, like parameters, conditions, and loops. You'll learn how to create reusable modules, automate deployments using CI/CD pipelines, and manage deployments across multiple environments. Real-world scenarios and practical examples are included to make your learning experience more meaningful and engaging. You'll learn how to use rollback and rollforward strategies to handle deployment failures smoothly. We'll also discuss Blue-Green Deployments, a strategy for reducing risk and downtime during updates.

Throughout this book, I'll provide troubleshooting techniques and solutions that have worked for me. By the end, you'll have a thorough understanding of Azure Bicep and be able to deploy Azure resources efficiently and confidently. So grab your laptop, launch your preferred text editor, and let's get started. Together, we'll realize Azure Bicep's full potential, transforming how you manage and deploy your infrastructure.

Welcome to the "Azure Bicep QuickStart Pro." Let us make Azure deployments simpler, faster, and more efficient.

Content

Preface

"**Azure Bicep QuickStart Pro**" is a handy reference for getting up and running with the Azure Bicep platform and deploying your first projects quickly and easily. Starting with the basics, this book walks you through the syntax of JSON and the templates available in Azure Resource Manager (ARM). With Bicep's declarative syntax and structure, you'll be up and running in no time, making infrastructure code management a breeze.

Parameters, conditions, and loops are some of the Bicep features that you will learn how to use to manage infrastructure deployments. Reusable module definition, decomposing complicated deployments into manageable components, and Bicep integration with CI/CD pipelines are all covered in the book. You will automate deployments and maintain consistency across development, staging, and production environments by utilizing GitHub Actions and Azure DevOps. To deal with deployment failures and minimize downtime, the book offers rollback and rollforward strategies, which are based on real-world problems. Additionally, Blue-Green Deployments are covered, which involve running two identical production environments to reduce risk during updates.

Managing dependencies, securely handling secrets, and monitoring and auditing your deployments are all within your reach with the help of practical solutions and troubleshooting techniques. When you finish this book, you will be able to confidently and efficiently deploy Azure resources.

In this book you will learn how to:

- Master Azure Bicep in no time, from the fundamentals to advanced deployment methods.
- Learn the ins and outs of Azure deployments using ARM templates written in JSON syntax.
- Efficiently manage your infrastructure by mastering Bicep's declarative syntax.
- Create a system of parameters, conditions, and loops to deploy resources dynamically.
- Decompose complex deployments into Bicep modules that can be reused.
- Create CI/CD pipelines to automate deployments with Azure DevOps and GitHub Actions.
- Distribute to various environments to ensure uniformity in staging, production, and development.
- Master the art of handling deployment failures with rollback and rollforward strategies.
- Make use of Blue-Green Deployments to reduce update risk.
- Use Azure Key Vault to safely store sensitive information in Bicep templates.

GitforGits

Prerequisites

You don't need any prior experience with cloud computing or Azure services to dive into this book; all you need is a solid grasp of cloud fundamentals. Knowledge of storage, compute, and networking is also preferred but not required.

Codes Usage

Are you in need of some helpful code examples to assist you in your programming and documentation? Look no further! Our book offers a wealth of supplemental material, including code examples and exercises.

Not only is this book here to aid you in getting your job done, but you have our permission to use the example code in your programs and documentation. However, please note that if you are reproducing a significant portion of the code, we do require you to contact us for permission.

But don't worry, using several chunks of code from this book in your program or answering a question by citing our book and quoting example code does not require permission. But if you do choose to give credit, an attribution typically includes the title, author, publisher, and ISBN. For example, "Azure Bicep QuickStart Pro by Selina Threxan".

If you are unsure whether your intended use of the code examples falls under fair use or the permissions outlined above, please do not hesitate to reach out to us at support@gitforgits.com.

We are happy to assist and clarify any concerns.

Acknowledgement

I owe a tremendous debt of gratitude to GitforGits, for their unflagging enthusiasm and wise counsel throughout the entire process of writing this book. Their knowledge and careful editing helped make sure the piece was useful for people of all reading levels and comprehension skills. In addition, I'd like to thank everyone involved in the publishing process for their efforts in making this book a reality. Their efforts, from copyediting to advertising, made the project what it is today.

Finally, I'd like to express my gratitude to everyone who has shown me unconditional love and encouragement throughout my life. Their support was crucial to the completion of this book. I appreciate your help with this endeavour and your continued interest in my career.

Chapter 1: Up and Running with ARM and JSON Syntax

Brief Introduction

In this chapter, I will walk you through the fundamental ideas behind Azure Resource Manager (ARM), as well as the JSON syntax that is utilized to define ARM templates. We will begin with a brief introduction to ARM, covering its purpose and the advantages it provides in managing Azure resources. You can automate deployment and configuration with ARM's consistent management layer, which brings a dependable and repeatable method to managing your Azure infrastructure.

We will go into the fundamentals of JSON syntax next. JSON is a simple data exchange format that both people and computers can easily understand and work with. You'll need to know how to define objects and arrays in order to create ARM templates, and I will show you examples and go over the rules of JSON to help you out. Once you have a good command of JSON, we can go on to creating simple ARM templates. I will demonstrate the process of making basic templates that specify Azure resources such as storage accounts, networking components, virtual machines, and virtual machines. In order to create adaptable and reusable templates, you will get an understanding of the various parts of an ARM template, such as parameters, variables, resources, and outputs.

At last, we'll go over the steps to use the Azure CLI to deploy ARM templates. Managing Azure resources is a breeze with the Azure CLI, a robust command-line tool that you can access from any terminal or command prompt. To deploy your ARM templates to Azure, I will show you how to install and configure the Azure CLI. Additionally, we will go over some standard procedures for structuring and organizing your JSON files so that your templates are both scalable and easy to maintain.

Overview of Azure Resource Manager (ARM)

Azure Resource Manager (ARM) is the deployment and management service for Azure. It provides a consistent management layer that allows you to create, update, and delete resources in your Azure account. ARM enables you to manage your infrastructure through declarative templates rather than scripts, ensuring a more predictable and manageable approach to deploying your cloud resources.

Key Concepts of ARM

Resource Groups

At the core of ARM is the concept of resource groups. A resource group is a container that holds related resources for an Azure solution. It includes every resource required for the solution, making it easy to manage and monitor them as a single entity. For example, all the resources for a web application, including the database, virtual machines, and networking components, can be placed in a single resource group.

Declarative Templates

ARM uses JSON-based templates to define the desired state of your infrastructure. These templates are human-readable files that specify the resources to be deployed and their configuration. This approach allows for consistent deployments, as the template can be version-controlled and reused across different environments.

Resource Providers

ARM uses resource providers to manage specific types of resources. Each resource type in Azure, such as virtual machines or storage accounts, has a corresponding resource provider. When you deploy a resource, ARM communicates with the appropriate resource provider to create and configure the resource according to your template.

Deployment Models

ARM supports both incremental and complete deployment models. Incremental deployments add or update resources defined in the template without affecting existing resources, while complete deployments delete resources that are not defined in the template. This flexibility allows you to choose the most suitable deployment strategy for your needs.

Tags

Tags are metadata you can add to your resources for organizational purposes. They consist of key-value pairs and can be used to categorize resources, making it easier to manage and query them. For example, you can tag resources by department, environment (development, staging, production), or project.

Role of ARM in Managing Azure Resources

ARM plays a pivotal role in managing Azure resources by providing a unified management layer that simplifies deployment, configuration, and maintenance. Given below is how ARM helps streamline resource management:

Consistent Deployment

With ARM, you can use templates to define the desired state of your infrastructure. This ensures that every deployment is consistent, reducing the chances of configuration drift and human error. Whether you are deploying to development, staging, or production, the same template can be used, ensuring that each environment is configured identically.

Dependency Management

ARM templates allow you to specify dependencies between resources. This ensures that resources are deployed in the correct order. For example, if a virtual machine depends on a storage account, ARM ensures that the storage account is created before the virtual machine.

Simplified Management

By grouping related resources in a resource group, ARM makes it easier to manage and monitor them as a single unit. You can perform bulk operations, such as starting or stopping all resources in a resource group, simplifying routine management tasks.

Role-Based Access Control (RBAC)

ARM integrates with Azure's RBAC system, allowing you to define granular access permissions for users and groups. This ensures that only authorized users can manage specific resources, enhancing security and compliance.

Policy Enforcement

ARM supports the creation and enforcement of policies to ensure compliance with organizational standards. You can define policies to control the types of resources that can be deployed, enforce naming conventions, or restrict resource locations. This helps maintain consistency and governance across your Azure environment.

How does ARM Works in Netflix-like?

To better understand how ARM works, we will consider a conceptual example involving a streaming service similar to Netflix. Imagine you are responsible for managing the infrastructure for this streaming service, which includes web servers, databases, content delivery networks (CDNs), and user authentication services. So now, you need to deploy a new version of the streaming service, which involves updating the web servers, adding a new database for user analytics, and configuring a CDN for faster content delivery.

To do this, you create a resource group named "StreamingService" to contain all the resources related to the streaming service. This includes virtual machines for web servers, Azure SQL Database for user data, Azure CDN for content delivery, and Azure Active Directory for user authentication. You define an ARM template that describes the desired state of the infrastructure. The template specifies the virtual machines, databases, CDN endpoints, and authentication services, along with their configurations. In the ARM template, you define dependencies between resources. For example, the web servers depend on the database and the CDN. ARM ensures that the database is created first, followed by the CDN, and finally, the web servers.

You then use the Azure CLI to deploy the ARM template. ARM processes the template, communicates with the appropriate resource providers, and orchestrates the creation and configuration of the resources in the correct order. Since the ARM template is version-controlled, you can easily deploy the same infrastructure to different environments (development, staging, production) with confidence that each environment will be identical. Apart from this, you define RBAC roles to ensure that only authorized team members can manage the resources in the "StreamingService" resource group. Additionally, you create policies to enforce naming conventions and restrict the deployment of resources to specific Azure regions. So at the end, you achieve a consistent, automated, and secure deployment process for the streaming service. It's conclusive that ARMs ability to use declarative templates, manage dependencies, and enforce policies makes it an essential tool for any organization using Azure.

Introduction to JSON Syntax

JSON (JavaScript Object Notation) is a lightweight data-interchange format that's easy for humans to read and write, and easy for machines to parse and generate. JSON is built on two structures: a collection of name/value pairs and an ordered list of values. These structures are universal, making JSON a flexible and powerful tool for data representation.

JSON Structure and Syntax Rules

Objects

Objects are enclosed in curly braces {} and consist of name/value pairs. Each name is followed by a colon : and the name/value pairs are separated by commas. The names (or keys) must be strings enclosed in double quotes, and the values can be strings, numbers, arrays, objects, true, false, or null.

```
{

  "name": "John Doe",

  "age": 30,

  "isStudent": false

}
```

Arrays

Arrays are ordered lists of values enclosed in square brackets `[]`. The values are separated by commas and can be of any type, including other arrays and objects.

```
[

  "apple",

  "banana",

  "cherry"
```

```
]
```

Values

JSON values can be of the following types:

- **String**: A sequence of characters enclosed in double quotes. For example: **`"hello"`**.
- **Number**: A numerical value without quotes. For example: **`123`** or **`45.67`**.
- **Boolean**: Either **`true`** or **`false`**.
- **Null**: A null value, written as **`null`**.
- **Object**: A JSON object enclosed in curly braces.
- **Array**: A JSON array enclosed in square brackets.

Strings

Strings must be enclosed in double quotes and can contain any Unicode character. Special characters must be escaped using a backslash ****.

For example:

```
"message": "Hello, \"World\"!"
```

JSON ignores whitespace around values, so you can use spaces, tabs, and newlines to format your JSON for readability.

Sample Program: Writing JSON Syntax

We will write a JSON representation for a simple ARM template that deploys a storage account in Azure. This practical example will help you understand the structure and syntax rules of JSON.

Define Storage Account Object

Start with the basic information required for the storage account.

```
{
  "type": "Microsoft.Storage/storageAccounts",
  "apiVersion": "2021-04-01",
  "name": "mystorageaccount",
```

```
  "location": "eastus",

  "sku": {

    "name": "Standard_LRS"

  },

  "kind": "StorageV2",

  "properties": {}

}
```

Wrap Storage Account Object in ARM Template Structure

ARM templates have a specific structure that includes sections for parameters, variables, resources, and outputs.

```
{

  "$schema":
"https://schema.management.azure.com/schemas/2019-04-01/deploymentTemplate.json#",

  "contentVersion": "1.0.0.0",

  "resources": [

    {

      "type": "Microsoft.Storage/storageAccounts",

      "apiVersion": "2021-04-01",

      "name": "mystorageaccount",

      "location": "eastus",

      "sku": {

        "name": "Standard_LRS"
```

```
      },
      "kind": "StorageV2",
      "properties": {}
    }
  ]
}
```

Add Parameters and Variables Sections

To make the template more flexible, add parameters for the storage account name and location. Variables can be used for fixed values or calculated settings.

```
{
  "$schema":
"https://schema.management.azure.com/schemas/2019-04-
01/deploymentTemplate.json#",
  "contentVersion": "1.0.0.0",
  "parameters": {
    "storageAccountName": {
      "type": "string"
    },
    "location": {
      "type": "string",
      "defaultValue": "eastus",
      "allowedValues": [
        "eastus",
```

```
        "westus",
        "centralus"
      ],
      "metadata": {
        "description": "Location of the storage account"
      }
    }
  },
  "variables": {},
  "resources": [
    {
      "type": "Microsoft.Storage/storageAccounts",
      "apiVersion": "2021-04-01",
      "name": "[parameters('storageAccountName')]",
      "location": "[parameters('location')]",
      "sku": {
        "name": "Standard_LRS"
      },
      "kind": "StorageV2",
      "properties": {}
    }
```

```
  ],
  "outputs": {}
}
```

Following is the breakdown of the above JSON template:

- **$schema**: Specifies the location of the JSON schema file that describes the version of the template language.
- **contentVersion**: A user-defined version number of the template.
- **parameters**: Defines the parameters that can be passed into the template. In this case, **`storageAccountName`** and **`location`**.
- **variables**: Defines variables that are used within the template. Currently empty in this example.
- **resources**: Specifies the resources to be deployed. In this case, a storage account.
- **outputs**: Defines the values that will be returned after the deployment. This is also currently empty in this example.

When you master the syntax and structure of JSON, you'll be able to make Azure deployment templates that are both dynamic and reusable. For consistent and dependable cloud environments, JSON is the best format for defining infrastructure as code because of its simplicity and readability.

Writing Basic ARM Templates

Azure Resource Manager (ARM) templates are JSON files that define the infrastructure and configuration for your Azure solution. They allow you to deploy, manage, and monitor all the resources for your solution as a group, ensuring consistency and repeatability. ARM templates are declarative, meaning you specify the desired state of your infrastructure, and Azure takes care of creating and configuring the resources to match that state.

ARM templates consist of several key components similar to the JSON template learned in the previous section. Now we shall create a simple ARM template that deploys a storage account in Azure. We will walk through each component and understand the structure of the template.

Define Template Structure

Start with the basic structure of an ARM template, including **`$schema`** and **`contentVersion`**.

```json
{
  "$schema":
"https://schema.management.azure.com/schemas/2019-04-01/deploymentTemplate.json#",
  "contentVersion": "1.0.0.0",
  "parameters": {},
  "variables": {},
  "resources": [],
  "outputs": {}
}
```

Add Parameters

Define parameters to make the template flexible. We will add parameters for the storage account name and location.

```json
{
  "$schema":
"https://schema.management.azure.com/schemas/2019-04-01/deploymentTemplate.json#",
  "contentVersion": "1.0.0.0",
  "parameters": {
    "storageAccountName": {
      "type": "string",
      "metadata": {
        "description": "Name of the storage account"
```

```
        }
      },
      "location": {
        "type": "string",
        "defaultValue": "eastus",
        "allowedValues": [
          "eastus",
          "westus",
          "centralus"
        ],
        "metadata": {
          "description": "Location of the storage account"
        }
      }
    },
    "variables": {},
    "resources": [],
    "outputs": {}
}
```

Add Variables

Define variables for values used within the template. We will add a variable for the storage account type.

```
{
  "$schema":
"https://schema.management.azure.com/schemas/2019-04-
01/deploymentTemplate.json#",
  "contentVersion": "1.0.0.0",
  "parameters": {
    "storageAccountName": {
      "type": "string",
      "metadata": {
        "description": "Name of the storage account"
      }
    },
    "location": {
      "type": "string",
      "defaultValue": "eastus",
      "allowedValues": [
        "eastus",
        "westus",
        "centralus"
      ],
      "metadata": {
        "description": "Location of the storage account"
```

```
      }
    }
  },
  "variables": {
    "storageAccountType": "Standard_LRS"
  },
  "resources": [],
  "outputs": {}
}
```

Define the Resource

Add the storage account resource to the **resources** section. Use the parameters and variables to configure the resource.

```
{
  "$schema":
"https://schema.management.azure.com/schemas/2019-04-
01/deploymentTemplate.json#",
  "contentVersion": "1.0.0.0",
  "parameters": {
    "storageAccountName": {
      "type": "string",
      "metadata": {
        "description": "Name of the storage account"
```

```
      }
    },
    "location": {
      "type": "string",
      "defaultValue": "eastus",
      "allowedValues": [
        "eastus",
        "westus",
        "centralus"
      ],
      "metadata": {
        "description": "Location of the storage account"
      }
    }
  },
  "variables": {
    "storageAccountType": "Standard_LRS"
  },
  "resources": [
    {
      "type": "Microsoft.Storage/storageAccounts",
```

```
      "apiVersion": "2021-04-01",
      "name": "[parameters('storageAccountName')]",
      "location": "[parameters('location')]",
      "sku": {
        "name": "[variables('storageAccountType')]"
      },
      "kind": "StorageV2",
      "properties": {}
    }
  ],
  "outputs": {}
}
```

Add Outputs

Define outputs to return values from the deployment. We will add an output to return the resource ID of the storage account.

```
{
  "$schema":
"https://schema.management.azure.com/schemas/2019-04-01/deploymentTemplate.json#",
  "contentVersion": "1.0.0.0",
  "parameters": {
    "storageAccountName": {
```

```
      "type": "string",
      "metadata": {
        "description": "Name of the storage account"
      }
    },
    "location": {
      "type": "string",
      "defaultValue": "eastus",
      "allowedValues": [
        "eastus",
        "westus",
        "centralus"
      ],
      "metadata": {
        "description": "Location of the storage account"
      }
    }
  },
  "variables": {
    "storageAccountType": "Standard_LRS"
  },
```

```
  "resources": [
    {
      "type": "Microsoft.Storage/storageAccounts",
      "apiVersion": "2021-04-01",
      "name": "[parameters('storageAccountName')]",
      "location": "[parameters('location')]",
      "sku": {
        "name": "[variables('storageAccountType')]"
      },
      "kind": "StorageV2",
      "properties": {}
    }
  ],
  "outputs": {
    "storageAccountResourceId": {
      "type": "string",
      "value":
"[resourceId('Microsoft.Storage/storageAccounts',
parameters('storageAccountName'))]"
    }
  }
}
```

By following this structure, you can create flexible and reusable ARM templates that automate the deployment and configuration of your Azure resources. ARM templates provide a powerful way to manage your infrastructure as code, ensuring consistency and reliability in your cloud environments.

Deploying ARM Templates

The Azure Command-Line Interface (CLI) is designed to manage Azure resources directly from the command line. In this section, I will go through setting up the Azure CLI on a Windows environment, introduce various commands and options used for deploying ARM templates, and demonstrate a practical deployment of an ARM template using the knowledge gained so far.

Setting up Azure CLI on Windows

Open your web browser and navigate to the Azure CLI download page: https://docs.microsoft.com/en-us/cli/azure/install-azure-cli-windows?tabs=azure-cli.

Click on the "Download" button to download the Azure CLI installer. Then, locate the downloaded installer file (typically named **AzureCLI.msi**) and double-click it to run the installer. Follow the on-screen instructions to complete the installation process. The default installation path is usually sufficient.

Open the Command Prompt or PowerShell and enter the following command to verify that the Azure CLI is installed correctly:

```
az --version
```

You should see output displaying the installed version of the Azure CLI along with other relevant details.

To start using the Azure CLI, you need to sign in to your Azure account. Run the following command:

```
az login
```

This command will open a web browser and prompt you to sign in with your Azure credentials. After signing in, you can close the browser window.

Azure CLI Commands and Options

The Azure CLI provides various commands and options to manage and deploy ARM templates. Given below are some essential commands you'll need:

Create a Resource Group

Before deploying an ARM template, create a resource group to contain the resources.

```
az group create --name myResourceGroup --location eastus
```

Validate the ARM Template

Validate the ARM template to ensure it is correctly formatted and all parameters are specified.

```
az deployment group validate --resource-group
myResourceGroup --template-file myTemplate.json --
parameters @myParameters.json
```

Deploy the ARM Template

Deploy the ARM template to the specified resource group.

```
az deployment group create --resource-group
myResourceGroup --template-file myTemplate.json --
parameters @myParameters.json
```

Check Deployment Status

Check the status of the deployment to see if it was successful.

```
az deployment group show --resource-group myResourceGroup
--name myDeployment
```

List Resources in a Resource Group

List all resources in a specific resource group.

```
az resource list --resource-group myResourceGroup
```

Delete a Resource Group

Delete a resource group and all the resources within it.

```
az group delete --name myResourceGroup --yes --no-wait
```

Deploying ARM Template

We will deploy the ARM template we created earlier, which defines a storage account, using the Azure CLI.

Create a Resource Group

First, create a resource group named **MyResourceGroup** in the **eastus** location.

```
az group create --name MyResourceGroup --location eastus
```

Prepare the ARM Template and Parameters File

Save the following ARM template as **storageAccountTemplate.json**:

```
{
  "$schema":
"https://schema.management.azure.com/schemas/2019-04-
01/deploymentTemplate.json#",
  "contentVersion": "1.0.0.0",
  "parameters": {
    "storageAccountName": {
      "type": "string",
      "metadata": {
        "description": "Name of the storage account"
      }
    },
    "location": {
      "type": "string",
      "defaultValue": "eastus",
```

```
        "allowedValues": [
          "eastus",
          "westus",
          "centralus"
        ],
        "metadata": {
          "description": "Location of the storage account"
        }
      }
    },
    "variables": {
      "storageAccountType": "Standard_LRS"
    },
    "resources": [
      {
        "type": "Microsoft.Storage/storageAccounts",
        "apiVersion": "2021-04-01",
        "name": "[parameters('storageAccountName')]",
        "location": "[parameters('location')]",
        "sku": {
          "name": "[variables('storageAccountType')]"
```

```
      },
      "kind": "StorageV2",
      "properties": {}
    }
  ],
  "outputs": {
    "storageAccountResourceId": {
      "type": "string",
      "value":
"[resourceId('Microsoft.Storage/storageAccounts',
parameters('storageAccountName'))]"
    }
  }
}
```

Save the following parameters file as **storageAccountParameters.json**:

```
{
  "$schema":
"https://schema.management.azure.com/schemas/2019-04-
01/deploymentParameters.json#",
  "contentVersion": "1.0.0.0",
  "parameters": {
    "storageAccountName": {
      "value": "mystorageaccount12345"
```

```
    },
    "location": {
      "value": "eastus"
    }
  }
}
```

Validate the ARM Template

Validate the template to ensure there are no errors.

```
az deployment group validate --resource-group
MyResourceGroup --template-file
storageAccountTemplate.json --parameters
@storageAccountParameters.json
```

If the validation is successful, you will see a message indicating that the template is valid.

Deploy the ARM Template

Deploy the template to the resource group.

```
az deployment group create --resource-group
MyResourceGroup --template-file
storageAccountTemplate.json --parameters
@storageAccountParameters.json
```

This command will initiate the deployment process. You can monitor the deployment status through the Azure portal or by using the CLI.

Check Deployment Status

Check the status of the deployment to confirm that the storage account has been created.

```
az deployment group show --resource-group MyResourceGroup
--name mystorageaccount12345
```

This command will display the details of the deployment, including any errors or warnings.

List Resources in the Resource Group

List all resources in the **`MyResourceGroup`** to verify that the storage account has been deployed.

```
az resource list --resource-group MyResourceGroup
```

You have now successfully deployed a storage account by utilizing an ARM template, gained knowledge of essential commands for managing ARM templates, and set up the Azure Command Line Interface (CLI) by following these steps.

Summary

To sum up, we began with exploring the foundational concepts of Azure Resource Manager (ARM) and JSON syntax. We began by understanding ARM's role in managing Azure resources, focusing on key concepts like resource groups, declarative templates, resource providers, deployment models, and tags. Through a conceptual example involving a Netflix-like streaming service, we illustrated how ARM simplifies resource management, ensures consistent deployments, and enhances security and compliance through role-based access control and policy enforcement.

Next, we delved into JSON syntax, learning about its structure and rules. We covered the basics of JSON objects and arrays, values, strings, and whitespace. A practical demonstration showed how to create a JSON representation for a simple ARM template, which helped solidify our understanding of JSON syntax and structure. We then moved on to writing ARM templates, starting with an overview of their components: $schema, contentVersion, parameters, variables, resources, and outputs. By creating a simple ARM template for deploying a storage account, we learned each component in detail, understanding their roles and how they fit together to define the desired state of Azure resources.

Finally, we learned how to deploy ARM templates using the Azure CLI. We set up the Azure CLI on a Windows environment, signed in to an Azure account, and explored various commands for managing and deploying ARM templates. We created a resource group, validated an ARM template, and deployed it using the Azure CLI. By the end of the chapter, we had a comprehensive understanding of how to use ARM templates and the Azure CLI to automate and manage Azure resource deployments, ensuring consistent and reliable infrastructure management.

Chapter 2: Getting Started with Bicep

Brief Introduction

Let us begin with our next chapter where we will dive into Bicep, a domain-specific language (DSL) for deploying Azure resources. Bicep simplifies the process of defining and managing your Azure infrastructure by providing a more readable and concise syntax compared to traditional JSON ARM templates. I will begin with an introduction to Bicep, exploring its key features, benefits, and how it enhances the deployment experience for Azure resources.

Next, I will set up the Bicep development environment in Visual Studio Code. This includes installing the necessary extensions and configuring the environment to enable efficient development and deployment of Bicep templates. I will teach you through each step to ensure your setup is ready for creating and managing Bicep templates. With the environment set up, I will create our first Bicep template, focusing on understanding its syntax and structure. I will cover the essential elements of a Bicep template, such as parameters, variables, and resource declarations. This will provide a solid foundation for building more complex templates and leveraging Bicep's powerful features.

I will then explore how to convert existing ARM templates to Bicep, making it easier to transition from JSON to Bicep without starting from scratch. Finally, we will learn how to deploy Bicep templates using the Azure CLI, demonstrating the end-to-end process of defining, validating, and deploying Azure resources with Bicep. By the end of this chapter, you'll have a strong understanding of Bicep and be well-equipped to start using it for your Azure deployments.

Bicep Overview

Concept of Bicep

Bicep is a domain-specific language (DSL) for deploying Azure resources, designed to be a simpler and more concise alternative to JSON-based ARM templates. Azure Bicep offers a more intuitive way to define, deploy, and manage Azure infrastructure as code, making it easier for cloud professionals to work with complex deployments. Bicep is designed to improve readability and reduce the complexity inherent in JSON ARM templates, thereby enhancing the developer experience and reducing the potential for errors.

Bicep aims to streamline the infrastructure-as-code (IaC) process by providing a syntax that is both easy to write and understand. This makes it an attractive choice for both seasoned professionals and those new to cloud infrastructure. By abstracting away some of the complexities of ARM templates, Bicep enables users to focus more on defining their infrastructure needs rather than wrestling with syntax and structure.

Bicep for Cloud Professionals

For cloud professionals, Bicep plays a crucial role in simplifying the deployment and management of Azure resources. By providing a more user-friendly syntax, Bicep reduces the learning curve associated with ARM templates. This allows professionals to quickly become productive and efficient in defining infrastructure.

Bicep also supports modularity and reuse, which are essential for managing large and complex environments. Cloud professionals can break down their deployments into smaller, manageable pieces using Bicep modules, making it easier to maintain and update their infrastructure. Additionally, Bicep integrates seamlessly with existing Azure services and tools, ensuring that professionals can leverage their existing knowledge and workflows while benefiting from the enhanced capabilities of Bicep.

Comparing Bicep with ARM Templates

ARM templates have been the standard for defining Azure infrastructure as code. However, they have several limitations that Bicep aims to address. We will compare the two to understand the improvements Bicep brings to the table:

Readability

ARM templates are written in JSON, which can be verbose and difficult to read, especially for complex deployments. Bicep, on the other hand, uses a more concise and readable syntax that resembles programming languages. This makes it easier to understand the structure and content of the template at a glance.

Following is the snippet of the ARM template:

```
{

  "$schema":
"https://schema.management.azure.com/schemas/2019-04-
01/deploymentTemplate.json#",

  "contentVersion": "1.0.0.0",

  "resources": [

    {

      "type": "Microsoft.Storage/storageAccounts",

      "apiVersion": "2021-04-01",

      "name": "[parameters('storageAccountName')]",
```

```
      "location": "[parameters('location')]",
      "sku": {
        "name": "[variables('storageAccountType')]"
      },
      "kind": "StorageV2",
      "properties": {}
    }
  ]
}
```

And now see below the equivalent Bicep template:

```
resource storageAccount
'Microsoft.Storage/storageAccounts@2021-04-01' = {
  name: storageAccountName
  location: location
  sku: {
    name: storageAccountType
  }
  kind: 'StorageV2'
  properties: {}
}
```

Modularity

ARM templates can be challenging to modularize and reuse. While it is possible, the process is not as straightforward as it could be. Bicep introduces the concept of modules, allowing you to encapsulate and reuse pieces of infrastructure easily. This promotes better organization and reuse across different deployments.

Error Handling and Debugging

ARM templates can be difficult to debug due to their complexity and verbosity. Bicep provides better error messages and diagnostics, making it easier to identify and fix issues in your templates.

Tooling and Integration

While ARM templates are well-supported by Azure tools, Bicep is designed to integrate seamlessly with existing tools like Visual Studio Code, Azure CLI, and Azure Resource Manager. This ensures that you can leverage your existing workflows while benefiting from the improved syntax and features of Bicep.

Key Features of Bicep

Concise and Readable Syntax

Bicep's syntax is designed to be both concise and readable, making it easier to write and understand. This reduces the cognitive load on developers and helps prevent errors.

Given below is a quick example:

```
param storageAccountName string

param location string = 'eastus'

param storageAccountType string = 'Standard_LRS'


resource storageAccount
'Microsoft.Storage/storageAccounts@2021-04-01' = {

  name: storageAccountName

  location: location

  sku: {

    name: storageAccountType
```

```
  }
  kind: 'StorageV2'
  properties: {}
}
```

Modularity and Reuse

Bicep supports the creation of modules, which allow you to encapsulate and reuse pieces of infrastructure. This promotes better organization and makes it easier to manage large deployments.

Given below is a quick example:

```
module storageModule './storage.bicep' = {
  name: 'myStorage'
  params: {
    storageAccountName: 'mystorageaccount'
    location: 'eastus'
    storageAccountType: 'Standard_LRS'
  }
}
```

Type Safety and IntelliSense

Bicep includes type safety and IntelliSense support, which helps catch errors at compile time rather than at runtime. This feature significantly improves the development experience by providing real-time feedback and autocompletion as you write your templates.

Given below is a quick example:

```
param storageAccountName string
param location string = 'eastus'
```

```
param storageAccountType string = 'Standard_LRS'

resource storageAccount
'Microsoft.Storage/storageAccounts@2021-04-01' = {

  name: storageAccountName

  location: location

  sku: {

    name: storageAccountType

  }

  kind: 'StorageV2'

  properties: {}

}
```

Simplified Resource Declaration

Bicep simplifies the declaration of resources by reducing the boilerplate code required. This makes the templates easier to read and maintain.

Following is an example:

```
resource myStorageAccount
'Microsoft.Storage/storageAccounts@2021-04-01' = {

  name: storageAccountName

  location: location

  sku: {

    name: storageAccountType

  }
```

```
  kind: 'StorageV2'

  properties: {}

}
```

Automatic Dependency Management

Bicep automatically handles dependencies between resources. This means you don't need to manually define dependencies, which simplifies the template and reduces the potential for errors.

Following is an example:

```
resource vnet 'Microsoft.Network/virtualNetworks@2020-06-01' = {

  name: 'myVnet'

  location: location

  properties: {

    addressSpace: {

      addressPrefixes: [

        '10.0.0.0/16'

      ]

    }

  }

}


resource subnet
'Microsoft.Network/virtualNetworks/subnets@2020-06-01' =
{
```

```
  name: 'mySubnet'
  parent: vnet
  properties: {
    addressPrefix: '10.0.0.0/24'
  }
}
```

Integration with Azure CLI and Azure PowerShell

Bicep integrates seamlessly with Azure CLI and Azure PowerShell, allowing you to deploy Bicep files directly without needing to convert them to ARM templates first. This simplifies the deployment process and fits well with existing workflows.

Following is a sample CLI Command:

```
az deployment group create --resource-group
myResourceGroup --template-file main.bicep
```

Support for Expressions and Functions

Bicep supports a range of expressions and functions that allow you to perform calculations, manipulate strings, and reference resources dynamically. This makes the templates more powerful and flexible.

Following is an example:

```
param prefix string


var storageAccountName = '${prefix}storage'


resource storageAccount
'Microsoft.Storage/storageAccounts@2021-04-01' = {
  name: storageAccountName
```

```
  location: 'eastus'
  sku: {
    name: 'Standard_LRS'
  }
  kind: 'StorageV2'
  properties: {}
}
```

Through the utilization of these essential features, Bicep streamlines the procedure for establishing and overseeing Azure infrastructure, thereby increasing its accessibility and efficiency for cloud professionals. An enormous improvement over conventional ARM templates based on JSON is achieved by combining a short syntax with modularity, type safety, and easy integration with current tools.

Setting up Bicep in VS Code

Installing Visual Studio Code

Open your web browser and navigate to the Visual Studio Code download page: https://code.visualstudio.com/download. Click on the "Windows" download button to download the installer.

Locate the downloaded installer file (typically named **`VSCodeUserSetup-x64-<version>.exe`**) and double-click it to run the installer. Follow the on-screen instructions to complete the installation. You can choose the default options for most of the steps.

Once the installation is complete, launch Visual Studio Code by finding it in your Start menu or desktop shortcuts.

Adding Bicep Extension to Visual Studio Code

In Visual Studio Code, click on the Extensions icon in the Activity Bar on the side of the window. This will open the Extensions view.

In the Extensions view search bar, type "Bicep". Look for the extension named "Bicep" authored by Microsoft. Click the "Install" button next to the Bicep extension. This will install the extension and enable support for Bicep files in Visual Studio Code.

After installation, open a new file and save it with the **.bicep** extension. You should see syntax highlighting and other language features specific to Bicep, indicating that the extension is active.

Setting up the Development Environment

Open Command Prompt or PowerShell and enter the following command to check if Azure CLI is installed:

```
az --version
```

If Azure CLI is not installed, download and install it from: https://docs.microsoft.com/en-us/cli/azure/install-azure-cli-windows?tabs=azure-cli.

With Azure CLI installed, you can install Bicep CLI by running the following command:

```
az bicep install
```

Verify the installation by running:

```
az bicep version
```

Open Visual Studio Code and create a new directory for your Bicep project. You can do this by clicking on "File" > "Open Folder" and selecting or creating a new folder.

To enhance the Bicep development experience, you can configure some settings in Visual Studio Code. Open the settings by clicking on "File" > "Preferences" > "Settings". In the search bar, type "Bicep" and review the available settings. You can customize settings like validation, linting, and formatting according to your preferences.

To further enhance your development experience, consider installing extensions like "Azure Resource Manager (ARM) Tools" for additional Azure-related functionalities and "Prettier - Code Formatter" for consistent code formatting.

In the project directory, create a new file with the **.bicep** extension. For example, **main.bicep**. Open this file in Visual Studio Code and start writing your Bicep code. You should see features like syntax highlighting, IntelliSense, and error diagnostics provided by the Bicep extension.

When you are done with these steps, you'll have a fully functional Bicep development environment in Windows' Visual Studio Code. Now that you know how to use Bicep templates, you can begin building and managing Azure infrastructure.

Syntax and Structure of Bicep Template

While Bicep and ARM templates share the same fundamental concepts, Bicep enhances readability and reduces verbosity, making it easier to write and understand templates. We will dive into the syntax and structure of Bicep templates.

Basic Syntax of Bicep

Parameters

Parameters allow you to pass values into the template during deployment. This makes the template flexible and reusable.

```
param storageAccountName string

param location string = 'eastus'

param storageAccountType string = 'Standard_LRS'
```

Variables

Variables store values that are used within the template. These values can be calculated or set within the template.

```
var resourceGroupName = 'myResourceGroup'
```

Resources

Resources define the actual Azure services to be deployed. Each resource includes properties like type, API version, name, location, and specific configuration settings.

```
resource storageAccount
'Microsoft.Storage/storageAccounts@2021-04-01' = {

  name: storageAccountName

  location: location

  sku: {

    name: storageAccountType
```

```
  }
  kind: 'StorageV2'
  properties: {}
}
```

Outputs

Outputs return values from the deployed resources. These values can be used for further automation or displayed to the user.

```
output storageAccountResourceId string =
storageAccount.id
```

Creating a Standard Bicep Template

We will create a Bicep template to deploy a storage account, similar to the ARM template example we used in the previous chapter. To begin with, start with the basic structure of a Bicep template, including parameters, variables, resources, and outputs.

```
param storageAccountName string

param location string = 'eastus'

param storageAccountType string = 'Standard_LRS'


var resourceGroupName = 'myResourceGroup'


resource storageAccount
'Microsoft.Storage/storageAccounts@2021-04-01' = {

  name: storageAccountName

  location: location
```

```
  sku: {
    name: storageAccountType
  }
  kind: 'StorageV2'
  properties: {}
}

output storageAccountResourceId string =
storageAccount.id
```

In the above template,

1. **Parameters**:
    - **`storageAccountName`**: The name of the storage account to be created.
    - **`location`**: The location where the storage account will be deployed. Default is set to 'eastus'.
    - **`storageAccountType`**: The SKU (pricing tier) of the storage account. Default is set to 'Standard_LRS'.
2. **Variables**:
    - **`resourceGroupName`**: The name of the resource group. This is set to a fixed value 'myResourceGroup' for simplicity.
3. **Resources**:
    - **`storageAccount`**: This resource defines the storage account. The resource type is 'Microsoft.Storage/storageAccounts', and the API version is '2021-04-01'. The properties include the name, location, SKU, kind, and other configuration settings.
4. **Outputs**:
    - **`storageAccountResourceId`**: This output returns the resource ID of the deployed storage account.

Understanding Resources and Modules in Bicep

Resources

Resources in Bicep define the actual Azure services to be deployed. Each resource declaration includes the resource type, API version, name, location, and configuration properties.

Given below is a quick example:

```
resource storageAccount
'Microsoft.Storage/storageAccounts@2021-04-01' = {

  name: storageAccountName

  location: location

  sku: {

    name: storageAccountType

  }

  kind: 'StorageV2'

  properties: {}

}
```

In the above example,

- **`resource storageAccount 'Microsoft.Storage/storageAccounts@2021-04-01'`**: This declares a resource named **`storageAccount`** of type 'Microsoft.Storage/storageAccounts' with API version '2021-04-01'.
- **`name: storageAccountName`**: The name of the storage account, taken from the **`storageAccountName`** parameter.
- **`location: location`**: The location of the storage account, taken from the **`location`** parameter.
- **`sku`**: The SKU (pricing tier) of the storage account, taken from the **`storageAccountType`** parameter.

- **kind**: The kind of storage account, set to 'StorageV2'.
- **properties**: Additional properties for the storage account.

Modules

Modules in Bicep allow you to encapsulate and reuse pieces of infrastructure. This promotes better organization and reuse across different deployments. Creating a module involves defining a separate Bicep file for a specific piece of infrastructure and referencing it in your main template.

Given below is a quick example of creating a storage account module:

First, save the following code in a file named **storageAccount.bicep**:

```
param storageAccountName string

param location string = 'eastus'

param storageAccountType string = 'Standard_LRS'


resource storageAccount
'Microsoft.Storage/storageAccounts@2021-04-01' = {

  name: storageAccountName

  location: location

  sku: {

    name: storageAccountType

  }

  kind: 'StorageV2'

  properties: {}

}


output storageAccountResourceId string =
```

```
storageAccount.id
```

Create a main Bicep file and reference the module:

```
param storageAccountName string

param location string = 'eastus'

param storageAccountType string = 'Standard_LRS'


module storageModule './storageAccount.bicep' = {

  name: 'storageModuleDeployment'

  params: {

    storageAccountName: storageAccountName

    location: location

    storageAccountType: storageAccountType

  }

}


output storageAccountResourceId string =
storageModule.outputs.storageAccountResourceId
```

In this bicep file,

- **module storageModule './storageAccount.bicep'**: This declares a module named **storageModule** that references the **storageAccount.bicep** file.
- **name: 'storageModuleDeployment'**: The name of the module deployment.
- **params**: This section passes parameters from the main template to the module.

The **storageAccount** resource declaration encapsulates all the details needed to create and configure a storage account in Azure. This includes specifying the resource type, API version, name, location, SKU, kind, and any additional properties. By abstracting these details into a resource declaration, you can easily replicate and manage the deployment of storage accounts across different environments.

In our modules example, the **storageAccount.bicep** file represents a module that defines the storage account resource. By referencing this module in the main template, you can reuse the storage account definition across different projects and environments. This modular approach not only simplifies the management of individual resources but also promotes consistency and maintainability in your infrastructure code.

Sample Program: using Resources and Modules

Using a Simple Bicep Template

As done in the past, save the following code in a file named **main.bicep**:

```
param storageAccountName string

param location string = 'eastus'

param storageAccountType string = 'Standard_LRS'


resource storageAccount
'Microsoft.Storage/storageAccounts@2021-04-01' = {

  name: storageAccountName

  location: location

  sku: {

    name: storageAccountType

  }

  kind: 'StorageV2'

  properties: {}

}
```

```
output storageAccountResourceId string =
storageAccount.id
```

Use the following commands to deploy the Bicep template:

```
az group create --name myResourceGroup --location eastus

az deployment group create --resource-group
myResourceGroup --template-file main.bicep --parameters
storageAccountName=mystorageaccount123
```

Use the Azure portal or CLI to verify that the storage account has been created in the **`myResourceGroup`** resource group.

Creating and using a Module

Save the following code in a file named **`storageAccount.bicep`**:

```
param storageAccountName string

param location string = 'eastus'

param storageAccountType string = 'Standard_LRS'


resource storageAccount
'Microsoft.Storage/storageAccounts@2021-04-01' = {

  name: storageAccountName

  location: location

  sku: {

    name: storageAccountType

  }
```

```
  kind: 'StorageV2'
  properties: {}
}

output storageAccountResourceId string =
storageAccount.id
```

Save the following code in a file named **`main.bicep`**:

```
param storageAccountName string
param location string = 'eastus'
param storageAccountType string = 'Standard_LRS'

module storageModule './storageAccount.bicep' = {
  name: 'storageModuleDeployment'
  params: {
    storageAccountName: storageAccountName
    location: location
    storageAccountType: storageAccountType
  }
}

output storageAccountResourceId string =
storageModule.outputs.storageAccountResourceId
```

Use the following commands to deploy the main template, which references the module:

```
az group create --name myResourceGroup --location eastus

az deployment group create --resource-group
myResourceGroup --template-file main.bicep --parameters
storageAccountName=mystorageaccount123
```

With this Bicep template and the steps outlined here, you have defined a storage account and shown how to encapsulate and reuse infrastructure components using modules. It becomes much easier to manage complicated deployments with this modular approach, which improves the organization and maintainability of your infrastructure code.

Converting ARM Templates to Bicep

We will proceed with converting an existing ARM template to Bicep using the Bicep CLI. We will use a readily available ARM template from GitHub for this demonstration and continue to use this example throughout the rest of the chapters. For this demonstration, we'll use an ARM template that deploys a simple web application.

You can find this template on GitHub at the following URL: https://github.com/Azure/azure-quickstart-templates/tree/master/quickstarts/microsoft.storage/storage-account-create

You can download the **azuredeploy.json** file from the link above. And given below is how you convert this ARM template to Bicep using the Bicep CLI.

Download the ARM Template

Download the ARM template JSON file after navigating to the URL: https://github.com/Azure/azure-quickstart-templates/blob/master/quickstarts/microsoft.storage/storage-account-create/azuredeploy.json

Use the Bicep CLI to decompile the ARM template JSON file into a Bicep file using the following command:

```
az bicep decompile --file azuredeploy.json
```

This command will generate a Bicep file (**azuredeploy.bicep**) in the same directory.

Sample ARM Template (azuredeploy.json)

Given below is the ARM template we will convert:

```
{
  "$schema":
"https://schema.management.azure.com/schemas/2019-04-
01/deploymentTemplate.json#",
  "contentVersion": "1.0.0.0",
  "parameters": {
    "storageAccountType": {
      "type": "string",
      "defaultValue": "Standard_LRS",
      "allowedValues": [
        "Standard_LRS",
        "Standard_GRS",
        "Standard_RAGRS",
        "Standard_ZRS",
        "Premium_LRS",
        "Premium_ZRS"
      ],
      "metadata": {
        "description": "Storage Account type"
      }
    },
    "location": {
```

```
      "type": "string",
      "defaultValue": "[resourceGroup().location]",
      "metadata": {
        "description": "Location for the Storage Account"
      }
    }
  },
  "resources": [
    {
      "type": "Microsoft.Storage/storageAccounts",
      "apiVersion": "2019-04-01",
      "name": "[concat('storage',
uniqueString(resourceGroup().id))]",
      "location": "[parameters('location')]",
      "sku": {
        "name": "[parameters('storageAccountType')]"
      },
      "kind": "StorageV2",
      "properties": {}
    }
  ],
  "outputs": {
```

```
    "storageAccountName": {
      "type": "string",
      "value": "[concat('storage',
uniqueString(resourceGroup().id))]"
    }
  }
}
```

Converted Bicep Template (azuredeploy.bicep)

Now, below is what the Bicep file might look like after conversion:

```
param storageAccountType string = 'Standard_LRS' {
  allowed: [
    'Standard_LRS'
    'Standard_GRS'
    'Standard_RAGRS'
    'Standard_ZRS'
    'Premium_LRS'
    'Premium_ZRS'
  ]
  metadata: {
    description: 'Storage Account type'
  }
}
```

```
param location string = resourceGroup().location {
  metadata: {
    description: 'Location for the Storage Account'
  }
}

resource storageAccount
'Microsoft.Storage/storageAccounts@2019-04-01' = {
  name: 'storage${uniqueString(resourceGroup().id)}'
  location: location
  sku: {
    name: storageAccountType
  }
  kind: 'StorageV2'
  properties: {}
}

output storageAccountName string = storageAccount.name
```

Now, to use the converted bicep template,

- Open Visual Studio Code and navigate to the directory where the **azuredeploy.bicep** file is located. Open the **azuredeploy.bicep** file.
- The Bicep file contains parameters for **storageAccountType** and **location**. It

defines a resource for the storage account (**Microsoft.Storage/storageAccounts**).

- **storageAccountType**: Specifies the type of storage account to be created.
- **location**: Specifies the location where the storage account will be deployed.

- Use the Azure CLI to deploy the Bicep template and run the following commands:

```
az group create --name myResourceGroup --location eastus

az deployment group create --resource-group
myResourceGroup --template-file azuredeploy.bicep --
parameters storageAccountType=Standard_LRS
```

- Now here,
  - **az group create** creates a resource group named **myResourceGroup** in the **eastus** location.
  - **az deployment group create** command deploys the Bicep template to the specified resource group, passing the **storageAccountType** parameter.

After deployment, you can verify the resources created by checking the Azure portal or using the Azure CLI to list the resources in the resource group:

```
az resource list --resource-group myResourceGroup
```

By using this example throughout the rest of the chapters, you'll be able to build upon this foundation to use Azure Bicep for deployments.

Summary

Just to summarize, I explored the basics of Bicep, a domain-specific language for deploying Azure resources. I started by understanding the concept of Bicep and its role in simplifying infrastructure as code for cloud professionals. Then, I set up the Bicep development environment in Visual Studio Code, which involved installing the necessary extensions and configuring the environment. This setup ensured that I had the tools needed to create and manage Bicep templates effectively. I then created my first Bicep template, focusing on the syntax and structure, which included defining parameters, variables, resources, and outputs. This exercise provided a clear understanding of how Bicep templates are organized and how they simplify the deployment process.

I learned how to convert existing ARM templates to Bicep using the Bicep CLI. This involved downloading an ARM template, using the Bicep CLI to decompile it, and examining the resulting Bicep file. The conversion process highlighted the improvements in readability and maintainability offered by Bicep. Finally, I deployed the converted Bicep template using the Azure CLI, reinforcing my understanding of the end-to-end deployment process. This hands-on experience demonstrated the practical benefits of using Bicep for Azure deployments, including easier management of infrastructure and reduced complexity. Overall, this chapter provided a comprehensive introduction to Bicep and equipped me with the skills to start using it effectively for my Azure projects.

CHAPTER 3: BICEP SYNTAX AND STRUCTURE

Brief Introduction

Welcome to chapter 3 wherein we'll explore a little deep into the syntax and structure of Bicep, so that we are strongly skilled in writing more effective and efficient templates for Azure deployments. We will start by understanding Bicep's declarative syntax, which simplifies the process of defining infrastructure by specifying the desired state rather than the steps to achieve that state. This approach makes templates more readable and easier to manage.

Next, we'll explore how to define resources in Bicep. Resources are the fundamental building blocks of your infrastructure, and we'll learn how to declare them, specify their properties, and organize them within your templates. This will provide a solid foundation for creating complex deployments. We will also cover the use of variables in Bicep. Variables allow you to store values that can be reused throughout your template, making it more concise and easier to maintain. You'll learn how to declare and reference variables, and how they can simplify your template structure.

Parameterizing Bicep templates is another crucial topic we'll address. Parameters make your templates flexible and reusable by allowing you to pass in values at deployment time. This enables you to customize your deployments without modifying the template itself. We will look at how to define parameters and use them effectively in your templates. Finally, we'll learn outputs in Bicep. Outputs allow you to return values from your deployments, which can be used for further automation or simply to provide information about the deployed resources. By the end of this chapter, you'll have a comprehensive understanding of Bicep's syntax and structure, enabling you to create robust and maintainable templates for your Azure infrastructure.

Understanding Bicep's Declarative Syntax

Overview

To get started with Bicep's declarative syntax, I need to understand that Bicep allows me to define the desired state of my Azure infrastructure without specifying the exact steps to achieve that state. This approach is different from imperative scripts, where I need to outline each step required to create and configure resources.

In Bicep, I write templates that describe what my infrastructure should look like, and Azure Resource Manager takes care of provisioning and configuring the resources to match that desired state. This makes the process more straightforward and less error-prone, as I don't need to manage the order of operations or handle intermediate states.

Comparing Bicep with Imperative Scripts

Now, we will compare Bicep's declarative approach with imperative scripting.

In an imperative script, I need to specify each step required to create and configure my resources.

This involves writing detailed commands and managing the order of operations. Given below is an example using Azure CLI:

```
# Create a resource group

az group create --name myResourceGroup --location eastus


# Create a storage account

az storage account create --name mystorageaccount --
resource-group myResourceGroup --location eastus --sku
Standard_LRS
```

In this script, I explicitly define each command and the sequence in which they must be executed. If there's an error in any step, I need to handle it manually and ensure that the subsequent steps can still proceed.

In contrast, Bicep allows me to declare the desired end state without worrying about the order of operations. Azure Resource Manager handles the provisioning and ensures that all dependencies are managed correctly. Given below is how the same resources are defined in Bicep:

```
param storageAccountName string

param location string = 'eastus'


resource storageAccount
'Microsoft.Storage/storageAccounts@2021-04-01' = {

  name: storageAccountName

  location: location

  sku: {

    name: 'Standard_LRS'

  }
```

```
  kind: 'StorageV2'

  properties: {}

}
```

I just say that I need a storage account with certain properties in this Bicep template. I don't have to keep track of the order of actions or write out each command. Azure handles managing dependencies and resource creation in the proper order. I can concentrate on specifying the intended state of my infrastructure rather than the specific actions to get there by using Bicep's declarative syntax. As a result, there is less chance of error and the deployment process as a whole is made simpler and my templates are easier to write, read, and maintain.

Using Variables in Bicep

In Bicep, variables allow me to store values that can be reused throughout the template. This helps in making the template more concise, readable, and easier to maintain. Variables can hold various types of data, including strings, integers, arrays, and objects. They can also be used to perform calculations and concatenations.

Declaring Variables

To declare a variable in Bicep, I use the **var** keyword followed by the variable name and its value. Following is the basic syntax for declaring a variable:

```
var <variableName> = <value>
```

I can declare variables for different data types, such as strings, integers, arrays, and objects. Given below are some examples:

String Variable

```
var storageAccountType = 'Standard_LRS'
```

Integer Variable

```
var numberOfInstances = 3
```

Array Variable

```
var locationList = [
  'eastus'
  'westus'
  'centralus'
]
```

Object Variable

```
var storageSku = {
  name: 'Standard_LRS'
  tier: 'Standard'
}
```

Using Variables in a Bicep Template

We will enhance our previous example by using variables. I will define variables to store values that I can reuse in the template.

Define Parameters

```
param storageAccountType string = 'Standard_LRS' {
  allowed: [
    'Standard_LRS'
    'Standard_GRS'
    'Standard_RAGRS'
    'Standard_ZRS'
```

```
    'Premium_LRS'
    'Premium_ZRS'
  ]
  metadata: {
    description: 'Storage Account type'
  }
}

param location string = resourceGroup().location {
  metadata: {
    description: 'Location for the Storage Account'
  }
}
```

Define Variables

Here, I declare variables for the storage account name and resource group ID concatenation.

```
var storageAccountPrefix = 'storage'
var uniqueStorageName =
'${storageAccountPrefix}${uniqueString(resourceGroup().id
)}'
```

Define the Resource

I use the variables **uniqueStorageName** and **storageAccountType** in the resource definition.

```
resource storageAccount
```

```
'Microsoft.Storage/storageAccounts@2019-04-01' = {
  name: uniqueStorageName
  location: location
  sku: {
    name: storageAccountType
  }
  kind: 'StorageV2'
  properties: {}
}
```

Define Outputs

I output the storage account name using the **uniqueStorageName** variable.

```
output storageAccountName string = storageAccount.name
```

Putting it all together, the complete Bicep template with variables looks like this:

```
param storageAccountType string = 'Standard_LRS' {
  allowed: [
    'Standard_LRS'
    'Standard_GRS'
    'Standard_RAGRS'
    'Standard_ZRS'
    'Premium_LRS'
    'Premium_ZRS'
```

```
  ]
  metadata: {
    description: 'Storage Account type'
  }
}

param location string = resourceGroup().location {
  metadata: {
    description: 'Location for the Storage Account'
  }
}

var storageAccountPrefix = 'storage'
var uniqueStorageName =
'${storageAccountPrefix}${uniqueString(resourceGroup().id
)}'

resource storageAccount
'Microsoft.Storage/storageAccounts@2019-04-01' = {
  name: uniqueStorageName
  location: location
  sku: {
```

```
    name: storageAccountType
  }
  kind: 'StorageV2'
  properties: {}
}

output storageAccountName string = storageAccount.name
```

The use of variables in Bicep has allowed me to streamline and improve the maintainability of my templates. I can carry out calculations, store and reuse values, and create increasingly intricate expressions inside of my templates thanks to variables.

Parameterizing Bicep Templates

What Are Parameters?

In Bicep, parameters allow me to pass values into my templates at deployment time. This makes my templates flexible and reusable because I can customize the deployment by providing different parameter values without changing the template itself. Parameters are defined at the beginning of a Bicep file and can be of various types, including strings, integers, booleans, arrays, and objects.

Parameters have several properties:

- **Type**: Specifies the type of the parameter (e.g., string, int, bool).
- **Default Value**: A value that is used if no value is provided during deployment.
- **Allowed Values**: A list of acceptable values for the parameter.
- **Metadata**: Provides additional information about the parameter, such as a description.

Creating Parameterized Templates

We will parameterize our existing Bicep template for creating a storage account. We will add parameters for the storage account name, location, and type. This will allow me to customize these values at deployment time.

Define Parameters

I start by defining parameters for the storage account name, location, and type.

```
param storageAccountName string {
  metadata: {
    description: 'The name of the storage account'
  }
}

param location string = 'eastus' {
  metadata: {
    description: 'The location for the storage account'
  }
}

param storageAccountType string = 'Standard_LRS' {
  allowed: [
    'Standard_LRS'
    'Standard_GRS'
    'Standard_RAGRS'
    'Standard_ZRS'
    'Premium_LRS'
    'Premium_ZRS'
```

```
  ]
  metadata: {
    description: 'The SKU of the storage account'
  }
}
```

In the above script,

- **storageAccountName**: This parameter will hold the name of the storage account.
- **location**: This parameter specifies the location where the storage account will be deployed. It has a default value of 'eastus'.
- **storageAccountType**: This parameter specifies the SKU of the storage account. It has a default value of 'Standard_LRS' and a list of allowed values.

Using Parameters in Resource Definitions

Next, I use these parameters in the resource definitions to customize the storage account properties based on the parameter values provided during deployment.

```
resource storageAccount
'Microsoft.Storage/storageAccounts@2019-04-01' = {
  name: storageAccountName
  location: location
  sku: {
    name: storageAccountType
  }
  kind: 'StorageV2'
  properties: {}
}
```

Outputs

I can also define outputs to return values from the deployment. For example, I can output the storage account name.

```
output storageAccountNameOutput string =
storageAccount.name
```

Putting it all together, the complete parameterized Bicep template looks like this:

```
param storageAccountName string {

  metadata: {

    description: 'The name of the storage account'

  }

}


param location string = 'eastus' {

  metadata: {

    description: 'The location for the storage account'

  }

}


param storageAccountType string = 'Standard_LRS' {

  allowed: [

    'Standard_LRS'

    'Standard_GRS'
```

```
    'Standard_RAGRS'

    'Standard_ZRS'

    'Premium_LRS'

    'Premium_ZRS'

  ]

  metadata: {

    description: 'The SKU of the storage account'

  }

}


resource storageAccount
'Microsoft.Storage/storageAccounts@2019-04-01' = {

  name: storageAccountName

  location: location

  sku: {

    name: storageAccountType

  }

  kind: 'StorageV2'

  properties: {}

}


output storageAccountNameOutput string =
```

```
storageAccount.name
```

Deploying Parameterized Templates

First, I create a resource group to hold the resources.

```
az group create --name myResourceGroup --location eastus
```

Next, I deploy the Bicep template, passing the parameter values.

```
az deployment group create \
  --resource-group myResourceGroup \
  --template-file azuredeploy.bicep \
  --parameters storageAccountName=mystorageaccount \
               location=westus \
               storageAccountType=Standard_GRS
```

In this command, I provide values for the **storageAccountName**, **location**, and **storageAccountType** parameters. The **location** parameter overrides the default value, while the **storageAccountType** parameter is set to **Standard_GRS**, one of the allowed values.

Using Parameter Files

Alternatively, I can use a parameter file to pass values to the Bicep template. This is especially useful for managing multiple parameters or sharing configurations.

Now to do this, I create a JSON file named **azuredeploy.parameters.json** with the following content:

```
{
  "$schema":
"https://schema.management.azure.com/schemas/2019-04-
01/deploymentParameters.json#",
  "contentVersion": "1.0.0.0",
```

```
  "parameters": {
    "storageAccountName": {
      "value": "mystorageaccount"
    },
    "location": {
      "value": "westus"
    },
    "storageAccountType": {
      "value": "Standard_GRS"
    }
  }
}
```

I use the Azure CLI to deploy the Bicep template, referencing the parameter file.

```
az deployment group create \
  --resource-group myResourceGroup \
  --template-file azuredeploy.bicep \
  --parameters @azuredeploy.parameters.json
```

The @ symbol before the file name tells the Azure CLI to use the file's content as parameter values. This particular method improves my infrastructure's scalability and maintainability as code solutions, allowing me to effectively oversee intricate Azure deployments.

Outputs in Bicep

Understanding Outputs

Outputs in Bicep allow me to return values from a deployment. These values can be used for further automation, to provide information about the deployed resources, or to pass data between different deployment stages. Outputs are defined at the end of a Bicep file and can include various types of data, such as strings, integers, arrays, and objects.

The syntax for defining an output is straightforward:

```
output <outputName> <outputType> = <value>
```

Here,

- **output**: The keyword used to define an output.
- **<outputName>**: A unique name for the output.
- **<outputType>**: The type of the output (e.g., string, int, bool).
- **<value>**: The value to be returned, which can be a static value or an expression referencing other resources or parameters.

Sample Program: using Outputs

We can continue using our previous example of a storage account to include outputs. I will define outputs to return the storage account name and the primary endpoint URL after the deployment.

Parameterized Bicep Template

Following is the updated Bicep template with added outputs:

```
param storageAccountName string {

  metadata: {

    description: 'The name of the storage account'

  }

}
```

```
param location string = 'eastus' {
  metadata: {
    description: 'The location for the storage account'
  }
}

param storageAccountType string = 'Standard_LRS' {
  allowed: [
    'Standard_LRS'
    'Standard_GRS'
    'Standard_RAGRS'
    'Standard_ZRS'
    'Premium_LRS'
    'Premium_ZRS'
  ]
  metadata: {
    description: 'The SKU of the storage account'
  }
}

resource storageAccount
'Microsoft.Storage/storageAccounts@2019-04-01' = {
```

```
  name: storageAccountName
  location: location
  sku: {
    name: storageAccountType
  }
  kind: 'StorageV2'
  properties: {}
}

output storageAccountNameOutput string =
storageAccount.name
output primaryEndpoints object =
storageAccount.properties.primaryEndpoints
```

Deploy the Bicep Template and Retrieve Outputs

To deploy this Bicep template and retrieve the outputs, I will use the Azure CLI.

First, I create a resource group to hold the resources.

```
az group create --name myResourceGroup --location eastus
```

Next, I deploy the Bicep template, passing the parameter values.

```
az deployment group create \
  --resource-group myResourceGroup \
  --template-file azuredeploy.bicep \
  --parameters storageAccountName=mystorageaccount \
```

```
                    location=westus \
                    storageAccountType=Standard_GRS
```

After the deployment, I can retrieve the outputs using the Azure CLI. The **--query** option helps me filter and display the output values.

```
az deployment group show \
  --resource-group myResourceGroup \
  --name mystorageaccount \
  --query properties.outputs
```

This command will return a JSON object containing the outputs defined in the Bicep template. For example:

```
{
  "storageAccountNameOutput": {
    "type": "String",
    "value": "mystorageaccount"
  },
  "primaryEndpoints": {
    "type": "Object",
    "value": {
      "blob":
"https://mystorageaccount.blob.core.windows.net/",
      "queue":
"https://mystorageaccount.queue.core.windows.net/",
      "table":
```

```
"https://mystorageaccount.table.core.windows.net/",
        "file":
"https://mystorageaccount.file.core.windows.net/"
      }
    }
}
```

This is particularly useful for chaining deployments, where the output of one deployment is used as input for another, or simply for gaining insights into the deployed infrastructure.

Summary

To summarize, I studied the syntax and structure of Bicep to gain a better understanding of how to build and manage Azure infrastructure. I started by looking into Bicep's declarative syntax, which allows me to define the desired state of my infrastructure without specifying the steps to get there. In comparison to imperative scripts, this approach improved template readability and management.

Next, I discovered how to define resources in Bicep. Resources are the basic building blocks of any Bicep template, representing a variety of Azure services. I looked at the syntax for resource definitions and learned common resource types like storage accounts, virtual networks, and virtual machines. By declaring resources, I was able to easily configure and deploy Azure services. I then went on to use variables in Bicep. Variables enabled me to save and reuse values throughout my template, making it more concise and maintainable. I practiced declaring variables and incorporating them into resource definitions, which made it easier to manage repeated values and complex expressions.

Parameters allowed me to pass values into the template during deployment, increasing flexibility and reusability. I learned how to define parameters with a variety of properties, including types, default values, allowed values, and metadata. This enabled me to customize deployments without changing the template itself. Finally, I learned outputs in Bicep, which enabled me to retrieve values from my deployments. Outputs provided useful information about the deployed resources, which could be used to automate or chain deployments. Overall, this chapter provided us with the knowledge and skills required to develop robust and maintainable Bicep templates for managing Azure infrastructure.

CHAPTER 4: ADVANCED BICEP FEATURES

Brief Introduction

The goal of this chapter is to explore Bicep's advanced features in more detail so that you can better manage complicated Azure deployments. These features give us more control and flexibility, so we can create more sophisticated and efficient templates. To begin with, I will look into using conditions in Bicep, which allow me to include or exclude resources based on certain criteria. This capability is required for developing dynamic templates that can adapt to various deployment scenarios. Next, I will learn how to use loops in Bicep to efficiently deploy multiple instances of a resource. Loops are especially useful for scaling applications and automating repetitive tasks. Next, I will concentrate on managing dependencies in Bicep. Proper dependency management ensures that resources are created in the correct order, reducing deployment errors and ensuring a smooth setup. I will understand how to define and manage these dependencies in my templates.

Securing my deployments is also critical, so I will go over how to securely manage secrets and sensitive data in Bicep. This includes integrating with Azure Key Vault and other security measures to protect sensitive information. Finally, I will learn error handling and debugging Bicep templates. Learning how to effectively identify and resolve errors will help me improve my development process and ensure consistent deployments. By the chapter's conclusion, I will have the knowledge and skills necessary to manage Azure deployments with greater complexity and agility, improving the safety and efficacy of my cloud infrastructure.

Using Conditions in Bicep

Concept of Conditions

Conditions in Bicep allow me to control the deployment of resources based on specific criteria. By using conditions, I can include or exclude resources dynamically, making my templates more flexible and adaptable to different deployment scenarios. Conditions are particularly useful when I want to deploy resources only under certain circumstances, such as deploying additional resources in a specific environment or based on user input.

In Bicep, I use the **`if`** keyword to define conditions. This keyword allows me to specify an expression that evaluates to true or false. If the expression evaluates to true, the resource is deployed; otherwise, it is skipped.

Sample Program: Conditional Resource Deployment

We continue with our previous example of deploying a storage account by adding a condition. We will add a parameter to control whether an additional resource, such as a Blob container, should be deployed alongside the storage account.

To begin with, I will start by defining a parameter to control the conditional deployment of the

Blob container.

```
param storageAccountName string {
  metadata: {
    description: 'The name of the storage account'
  }
}

param location string = 'eastus' {
  metadata: {
    description: 'The location for the storage account'
  }
}

param storageAccountType string = 'Standard_LRS' {
  allowed: [
    'Standard_LRS'
    'Standard_GRS'
    'Standard_RAGRS'
    'Standard_ZRS'
    'Premium_LRS'
    'Premium_ZRS'
```

```
  ]
  metadata: {
    description: 'The SKU of the storage account'
  }
}

param deployBlobContainer bool = false {
  metadata: {
    description: 'Condition to deploy Blob container'
  }
}
```

Here, **deployBlobContainer** is the boolean parameter that controls whether the Blob container should be deployed. It defaults to false.

Next, I will define the storage account resource and add a conditional Blob container resource using the **if** keyword.

```
resource storageAccount
'Microsoft.Storage/storageAccounts@2019-04-01' = {
  name: storageAccountName
  location: location
  sku: {
    name: storageAccountType
  }
  kind: 'StorageV2'
```

```
  properties: {}
}

resource blobContainer
'Microsoft.Storage/storageAccounts/blobServices/container
s@2019-04-01' = if (deployBlobContainer) {
  name: '${storageAccountName}/default/container01'
  properties: {}
}
```

In this, the **blobContainer** resource is deployed only if the **deployBlobContainer** parameter is true.

Coming to output, I can also define outputs to return information about the deployed resources.

```
output storageAccountNameOutput string =
storageAccount.name

output blobContainerNameOutput string =
blobContainer.name
```

Here, the **blobContainerNameOutput** will return the name of the Blob container if it is deployed.

Putting it all together, the complete Bicep template with conditions looks like this:

```
param storageAccountName string {
  metadata: {
    description: 'The name of the storage account'
  }
}
```

```
param location string = 'eastus' {
  metadata: {
    description: 'The location for the storage account'
  }
}

param storageAccountType string = 'Standard_LRS' {
  allowed: [
    'Standard_LRS'
    'Standard_GRS'
    'Standard_RAGRS'
    'Standard_ZRS'
    'Premium_LRS'
    'Premium_ZRS'
  ]
  metadata: {
    description: 'The SKU of the storage account'
  }
}
```

```
param deployBlobContainer bool = false {
  metadata: {
    description: 'Condition to deploy Blob container'
  }
}

resource storageAccount
'Microsoft.Storage/storageAccounts@2019-04-01' = {
  name: storageAccountName
  location: location
  sku: {
    name: storageAccountType
  }
  kind: 'StorageV2'
  properties: {}
}

resource blobContainer
'Microsoft.Storage/storageAccounts/blobServices/container
s@2019-04-01' = if (deployBlobContainer) {
  name: '${storageAccountName}/default/container01'
  properties: {}
```

```
}

output storageAccountNameOutput string =
storageAccount.name

output blobContainerNameOutput string =
blobContainer.name
```

Deploying the Template with Conditions

To deploy the above Bicep template and control the conditional deployment, I use the Azure CLI.

First, I create a resource group to hold the resources which are already learned in the previous chapter. I deploy the Bicep template without deploying the Blob container by setting the **deployBlobContainer** parameter to false (or by omitting it, as false is the default).

```
az deployment group create \

  --resource-group myResourceGroup \

  --template-file azuredeploy.bicep \

  --parameters storageAccountName=mystorageaccount \

               location=westus \

               storageAccountType=Standard_GRS
```

To deploy the Blob container along with the storage account, I set the **deployBlobContainer** parameter to true.

```
az deployment group create \

  --resource-group myResourceGroup \

  --template-file azuredeploy.bicep \

  --parameters storageAccountName=mystorageaccount \

               location=westus \
```

```
                    storageAccountType=Standard_GRS \

                    deployBlobContainer=true
```

It is possible to build dynamic templates that adjust to various deployment scenarios with the help of Bicep's conditions. As a result, I am able to better manage resources and adjust deployments to meet individual needs.

Implementing Loops in Bicep

Syntax of Loops

Loops in general, allows me to define multiple instances of resources, variables, or outputs by iterating over arrays and objects in Bicep. This is particularly useful for deploying multiple similar resources, such as creating multiple virtual machines or storage accounts. The syntax for loops in Bicep is straightforward and uses the **for** keyword to iterate over a collection.

The basic syntax for a loop in Bicep looks like this:

```
resource <resourceName> '<resourceType>@<apiVersion>' =
[for <item> in <array>: {

  // Resource properties

}]
```

Here, **for <item> in <array>** defines the loop, where **<item>** is the current item in the iteration, and **<array>** is the collection being iterated over.

Sample Program: Iterating Over Arrays and Objects

We will try to enhance our storage account example by creating multiple storage accounts using loops. I will define an array of storage account names and use a loop to create a storage account for each name in the array.

I will start by defining a parameter for the storage account type and an array variable for the storage account names.

```
param storageAccountType string = 'Standard_LRS' {

  allowed: [
```

```
    'Standard_LRS'
    'Standard_GRS'
    'Standard_RAGRS'
    'Standard_ZRS'
    'Premium_LRS'
    'Premium_ZRS'
  ]
  metadata: {
    description: 'The SKU of the storage account'
  }
}

param location string = 'eastus' {
  metadata: {
    description: 'The location for the storage account'
  }
}

var storageAccountNames = [
  'storageaccount01'
  'storageaccount02'
```

```
  'storageaccount03'

]
```

In the above example,

- **storageAccountType**: This parameter specifies the SKU of the storage account.
- **location**: This parameter specifies the location where the storage accounts will be deployed.
- **storageAccountNames**: This variable is an array of storage account names.

Next, I will use a loop to create a storage account for each name in the **storageAccountNames** array.

```
resource storageAccounts
'Microsoft.Storage/storageAccounts@2019-04-01' = [for
accountName in storageAccountNames: {

  name: accountName

  location: location

  sku: {

    name: storageAccountType

  }

  kind: 'StorageV2'

  properties: {}

}]
```

In the above example, the loop iterates over each name in the **storageAccountNames** array, creating a storage account with the specified properties.

I can also define outputs to return the names of the created storage accounts.

```
output storageAccountNamesOutput array = [for account in
storageAccounts: account.name]
```

This output returns an array of storage account names created by the loop. Putting it all together, the complete Bicep template with loops looks like this:

```
param storageAccountType string = 'Standard_LRS' {

  allowed: [

    'Standard_LRS'

    'Standard_GRS'

    'Standard_RAGRS'

    'Standard_ZRS'

    'Premium_LRS'

    'Premium_ZRS'

  ]

  metadata: {

    description: 'The SKU of the storage account'

  }

}


param location string = 'eastus' {

  metadata: {

    description: 'The location for the storage account'

  }

}
```

```
var storageAccountNames = [
  'storageaccount01'
  'storageaccount02'
  'storageaccount03'
]

resource storageAccounts
'Microsoft.Storage/storageAccounts@2019-04-01' = [for
accountName in storageAccountNames: {
  name: accountName
  location: location
  sku: {
    name: storageAccountType
  }
  kind: 'StorageV2'
  properties: {}
}]

output storageAccountNamesOutput array = [for account in
storageAccounts: account.name]
```

Deploying the Template with Loops

Next, I deploy the Bicep template, passing the parameter values.

```
az deployment group create \
  --resource-group myResourceGroup \
  --template-file azuredeploy.bicep \
  --parameters location=westus \
               storageAccountType=Standard_GRS
```

This deployment will create three storage accounts named **storageaccount01**, **storageaccount02**, and **storageaccount03** in the specified location and with the specified SKU.

Handling Dependencies

The proper sequence of resource creation is guaranteed in Bicep by careful dependency management. To deal with situations where one resource relies on another, Bicep allows for the explicit definition of dependencies. In complicated deployments, this is of the utmost importance because resources must be available before they can be created.

Defining and Managing Dependencies

To define dependencies in Bicep, I use the **dependsOn** property. This property explicitly states that a resource depends on one or more other resources.

Given below is the syntax:

```
resource <resourceName> '<resourceType>@<apiVersion>' = {
  name: <resourceName>
  location: <location>
  properties: {
    // resource properties
  }
  dependsOn: [
```

```
    <resourceName1>
    <resourceName2>
  ]
}
```

Sample Program: Deploying Virtual Machine

Think of a situation where I need to create a storage account and a virtual machine. The virtual machine should be deployed only after the storage account is available. To begin with, I will start by defining the storage account and virtual machine resources, specifying the dependency.

```
param location string = 'eastus'


resource storageAccount
'Microsoft.Storage/storageAccounts@2019-04-01' = {
  name: 'mystorageaccount'
  location: location
  sku: {
    name: 'Standard_LRS'
  }
  kind: 'StorageV2'
  properties: {}
}


resource vm 'Microsoft.Compute/virtualMachines@2021-03-
01' = {
```

```
  name: 'myVM'
  location: location
  properties: {
    hardwareProfile: {
      vmSize: 'Standard_DS1_v2'
    }
    storageProfile: {
      osDisk: {
        createOption: 'FromImage'
      }
      imageReference: {
        publisher: 'Canonical'
        offer: 'UbuntuServer'
        sku: '18.04-LTS'
        version: 'latest'
      }
    }
    osProfile: {
      computerName: 'myVM'
      adminUsername: 'azureuser'
      adminPassword: 'P@ssword1234'
```

```
    }
    networkProfile: {
      networkInterfaces: [
        {
          id: '/subscriptions/<subscription-
id>/resourceGroups/myResourceGroup/providers/Microsoft.Ne
twork/networkInterfaces/myNic'
        }
      ]
    }
  }
  dependsOn: [
    storageAccount
  ]
}
```

Here, the **vm** resource depends on the **storageAccount** resource. This ensures that the virtual machine is deployed only after the storage account is created.

Scenario 1: Circular Dependencies

A circular dependency occurs when two or more resources depend on each other. This creates a loop that Azure Resource Manager cannot resolve. For example, if a virtual machine depends on a network interface, and the network interface depends on the virtual machine, a circular dependency is created.

In order to break the circular dependency, it can be done only by re-evaluating the resource relationships. Often, refactoring the deployment architecture can help avoid such loops.

```
resource networkInterface
```

```
'Microsoft.Network/networkInterfaces@2021-03-01' = {
  name: 'myNic'
  location: location
  properties: {
    ipConfigurations: [
      {
        name: 'ipConfig1'
        properties: {
          privateIPAllocationMethod: 'Dynamic'
          subnet: {
            id: '/subscriptions/<subscription-
id>/resourceGroups/myResourceGroup/providers/Microsoft.Ne
twork/virtualNetworks/myVnet/subnets/default'
          }
        }
      }
    ]
  }
}

resource vm 'Microsoft.Compute/virtualMachines@2021-03-
01' = {
  name: 'myVM'
```

```
location: location
properties: {
  hardwareProfile: {
    vmSize: 'Standard_DS1_v2'
  }
  storageProfile: {
    osDisk: {
      createOption: 'FromImage'
    }
    imageReference: {
      publisher: 'Canonical'
      offer: 'UbuntuServer'
      sku: '18.04-LTS'
      version: 'latest'
    }
  }
  osProfile: {
    computerName: 'myVM'
    adminUsername: 'azureuser'
    adminPassword: 'P@ssword1234'
  }
```

```
    networkProfile: {
      networkInterfaces: [
        {
          id: networkInterface.id
        }
      ]
    }
  }
  dependsOn: [
    networkInterface
  ]
}
```

Scenario 2: Complex Dependencies with Multiple Levels

In complex deployments, resources might depend on several other resources across multiple levels. For example, a virtual machine might depend on a network interface, which in turn depends on a virtual network and a subnet.

Now to overcome this, use **dependsOn** to define multi-level dependencies clearly. Ensure each resource is created in the necessary order by listing all required dependencies.

```
resource vnet 'Microsoft.Network/virtualNetworks@2021-02-01' = {
  name: 'myVnet'
  location: location
  properties: {
```

```
    addressSpace: {
      addressPrefixes: [
        '10.0.0.0/16'
      ]
    }
  }
}

resource subnet
'Microsoft.Network/virtualNetworks/subnets@2021-02-01' =
{
  name: 'mySubnet'
  parent: vnet
  properties: {
    addressPrefix: '10.0.0.0/24'
  }
}

resource networkInterface
'Microsoft.Network/networkInterfaces@2021-02-01' = {
  name: 'myNic'
  location: location
```

```
  properties: {
    ipConfigurations: [
      {
        name: 'ipConfig1'
        properties: {
          privateIPAllocationMethod: 'Dynamic'
          subnet: {
            id: subnet.id
          }
        }
      }
    ]
  }
  dependsOn: [
    subnet
  ]
}

resource vm 'Microsoft.Compute/virtualMachines@2021-03-
01' = {
  name: 'myVM'
  location: location
```

```
properties: {
  hardwareProfile: {
    vmSize: 'Standard_DS1_v2'
  }
  storageProfile: {
    osDisk: {
      createOption: 'FromImage'
    }
    imageReference: {
      publisher: 'Canonical'
      offer: 'UbuntuServer'
      sku: '18.04-LTS'
      version: 'latest'
    }
  }
  osProfile: {
    computerName: 'myVM'
    adminUsername: 'azureuser'
    adminPassword: 'P@ssword1234'
  }
  networkProfile: {
```

```
        networkInterfaces: [
          {
            id: networkInterface.id
          }
        ]
      }
    }
    dependsOn: [
      networkInterface
    ]
}
```

In the above code snippet, the **vm** resource depends on **networkInterface**, which depends on **subnet**, which in turn depends on **vnet**. Each resource is created in the correct order, ensuring a successful deployment.

Overall, you can avoid mistakes and make sure everything goes smoothly during deployment by learning about and managing dependencies in Bicep. This will guarantee that resources are deployed in the right order. For complicated deployments, this method is vital because the sequence of resource creation matters a great deal.

Securely Managing Secrets and Sensitive Data

Azure Key Vault Overview

The Azure Key Vault service is a cloud-based application that offers safe storage for certificates, keys, and any other confidential information. You can protect sensitive information with industry-standard algorithms, hardware security modules (HSMs), and access control policies by utilizing Azure Key Vault. This allows me to centralize the storage of application secrets and protect sensitive information. Cryptographic keys and secrets that are utilized by cloud applications and services can be protected with the assistance of Key Vault, which also offers secure access and management mechanisms.

In Bicep, I can integrate with Azure Key Vault to retrieve secrets and use them in my deployments. This allows me to avoid hardcoding sensitive information, such as passwords or API keys, directly in the Bicep templates. Instead, I store these secrets in Key Vault and reference them securely.

Sample Program: Secrets Management with Azure Key Vault

To begin with, I will create an Azure Key Vault and store a secret in it.

```
# Create a resource group for the Key Vault

az group create --name myKeyVaultResourceGroup --location eastus



# Create the Key Vault

az keyvault create --name myKeyVault --resource-group myKeyVaultResourceGroup --location eastus



# Store a secret in the Key Vault

az keyvault secret set --vault-name myKeyVault --name mySecret --value mySecretValue123
```

Next, I will define a Bicep template that retrieves the secret from the Key Vault and uses it in a resource deployment.

```
param keyVaultName string

param secretName string

param location string = 'eastus'



resource keyVault 'Microsoft.KeyVault/vaults@2019-09-01' existing = {
```

```
  name: keyVaultName
}

resource secret 'Microsoft.KeyVault/vaults/secrets@2019-
09-01' existing = {
  parent: keyVault
  name: secretName
}

var secretValue = secret.properties.value

resource storageAccount
'Microsoft.Storage/storageAccounts@2019-04-01' = {
  name: 'mystorageaccount'
  location: location
  sku: {
    name: 'Standard_LRS'
  }
  kind: 'StorageV2'
  properties: {
    encryption: {
      keySource: 'Microsoft.Keyvault'
```

```
      keyVaultProperties: {
        keyVaultUri: keyVault.properties.vaultUri
        keyName: secretName
        keyVersion: secret.properties.latestVersion
      }
    }
  }
}

output secretValueOutput string = secretValue
```

I will use the Azure CLI to deploy the Bicep template and retrieve the secret from Key Vault.

```
# Create a resource group for the deployment
az group create --name myResourceGroup --location eastus

# Deploy the Bicep template
az deployment group create \
  --resource-group myResourceGroup \
  --template-file azuredeploy.bicep \
  --parameters keyVaultName=myKeyVault
secretName=mySecret location=eastus
```

This deployment retrieves the secret **mySecret** from the Key Vault **myKeyVault** and uses it in the deployment of a storage account. The **secretValue** variable holds the value of the secret, and it is used in the properties of the storage account.

Error Handling and Debugging

Common Errors and Issues

When working with Bicep templates, I may encounter various errors and issues related to syntax, missing parameters, resource conflicts, and dependencies. These errors can arise during template validation, deployment, or runtime.

Common issues include:

- Mistakes in the Bicep code, such as missing brackets, incorrect parameter types, or typos, can cause syntax errors.
- If a required parameter is not provided or is incorrectly named, the deployment will fail.
- Deploying resources with conflicting names or configurations can cause conflicts.
- Incorrectly defined or missing dependencies can lead to deployment failures.

To improve my debugging experience with Bicep, I can use the Azure Resource Manager (ARM) tools and extensions in Visual Studio Code. These tools provide features like syntax highlighting, IntelliSense, and validation, making it easier to identify and fix errors in my Bicep templates.

Following are the Visual Studio Code extensions:

- **Bicep Extension**: Provides syntax highlighting, IntelliSense, and real-time validation for Bicep files.
- **Azure Resource Manager Tools**: Enhances the development experience with ARM templates and Bicep, offering advanced features like template outline, parameter file matching, and deployment validation.

Practical Solutions to Error Handling

Syntax Error

Let us say that a common syntax error occurs when I forget to close a bracket or misplace a comma in the following script:

```
param storageAccountName string

param location string = 'eastus'
```

```
resource storageAccount
'Microsoft.Storage/storageAccounts@2021-04-01' = {

  name: storageAccountName

  location: location

  sku: {

    name: 'Standard_LRS'

  }

  kind: 'StorageV2'

  properties: {}
```

In the above code snippet, the closing bracket for the **storageAccount** resource is missing.

To address this issue, use the Bicep extension in Visual Studio Code to identify and fix the syntax error. The extension highlights the error and provides suggestions for correction.

Following is the corrected script:

```
param storageAccountName string

param location string = 'eastus'


resource storageAccount
'Microsoft.Storage/storageAccounts@2021-04-01' = {

  name: storageAccountName

  location: location

  sku: {

    name: 'Standard_LRS'

  }
```

```
  kind: 'StorageV2'

  properties: {}

}
```

Missing Parameter

Let us consider that the deployment has failed if a required parameter is missing or incorrectly named in the following snippet.

```
param storageAccountName string

param location string = 'eastus'


resource storageAccount
'Microsoft.Storage/storageAccounts@2021-04-01' = {

  name: storageAccountName

  location: location

  sku: {

    name: 'Standard_LRS'

  }

  kind: 'StorageV2'

  properties: {}

}
```

When deploying this template, I might forget to provide the **storageAccountName** parameter.

Now, to resolve this, first ensure all required parameters are provided during deployment. I can validate the template before deployment using the Azure CLI.

```
az deployment group validate --resource-group
myResourceGroup --template-file azuredeploy.bicep --
parameters storageAccountName=mystorageaccount
```

This command checks for missing parameters and other issues before the actual deployment.

Resource Conflict

Another common issue is about resource conflicts, which can occur if I attempt to deploy resources with the same name in the same resource group.

```
param storageAccountName string

param location string = 'eastus'


resource storageAccount1
'Microsoft.Storage/storageAccounts@2021-04-01' = {

  name: storageAccountName

  location: location

  sku: {

    name: 'Standard_LRS'

  }

  kind: 'StorageV2'

  properties: {}

}


resource storageAccount2
'Microsoft.Storage/storageAccounts@2021-04-01' = {
```

```
  name: storageAccountName
  location: location
  sku: {
    name: 'Standard_LRS'
  }
  kind: 'StorageV2'
  properties: {}
}
```

Both **storageAccount1** and **storageAccount2** have the same name, causing a conflict. In order to resolve this, use unique names for each resource to avoid conflicts. I can use the **uniqueString** function to generate unique names based on the resource group ID.

Following is the corrected code:

```
param storageAccountNamePrefix string

param location string = 'eastus'


resource storageAccount1
'Microsoft.Storage/storageAccounts@2021-04-01' = {
  name:
'${storageAccountNamePrefix}1${uniqueString(resourceGroup
().id)}'
  location: location
  sku: {
    name: 'Standard_LRS'
  }
```

```
  kind: 'StorageV2'

  properties: {}

}


resource storageAccount2
'Microsoft.Storage/storageAccounts@2021-04-01' = {

  name:
'${storageAccountNamePrefix}2${uniqueString(resourceGroup
().id)}'

  location: location

  sku: {

    name: 'Standard_LRS'

  }

  kind: 'StorageV2'

  properties: {}

}
```

Dependency Issue

Another common problem that may occur is that the deployment can fail if dependencies are not correctly defined, causing resources to be created in the wrong order. Following is a quick example:

```
param location string = 'eastus'


resource network 'Microsoft.Network/virtualNetworks@2021-
02-01' = {
```

```
  name: 'myVnet'
  location: location
  properties: {
    addressSpace: {
      addressPrefixes: [
        '10.0.0.0/16'
      ]
    }
  }
}

resource subnet
'Microsoft.Network/virtualNetworks/subnets@2021-02-01' =
{
  name: 'mySubnet'
  parent: network
  properties: {
    addressPrefix: '10.0.0.0/24'
  }
}

resource vm 'Microsoft.Compute/virtualMachines@2021-03-
```

```
01' = {
  name: 'myVM'
  location: location
  properties: {
    hardwareProfile: {
      vmSize: 'Standard_DS1_v2'
    }
    storageProfile: {
      osDisk: {
        createOption: 'FromImage'
      }
      imageReference: {
        publisher: 'Canonical'
        offer: 'UbuntuServer'
        sku: '18.04-LTS'
        version: 'latest'
      }
    }
    osProfile: {
      computerName: 'myVM'
      adminUsername: 'azureuser'
```

```
      adminPassword: 'P@ssword1234'
    }
    networkProfile: {
      networkInterfaces: [
        {
          id: '/subscriptions/<subscription-
id>/resourceGroups/myResourceGroup/providers/Microsoft.Ne
twork/networkInterfaces/myNic'
        }
      ]
    }
  }
}
```

The virtual machine depends on a network interface, but the network interface resource is not defined. Additionally, the VM should depend on the subnet. To address this issue, first define the missing network interface resource and set up correct dependencies as shown below:

```
param location string = 'eastus'

resource network 'Microsoft.Network/virtualNetworks@2021-
02-01' = {
  name: 'myVnet'
  location: location
  properties: {
```

```
    addressSpace: {
      addressPrefixes: [
        '10.0.0.0/16'
      ]
    }
  }
}

resource subnet
'Microsoft.Network/virtualNetworks/subnets@2021-02-01' =
{
  name: 'mySubnet'
  parent: network
  properties: {
    addressPrefix: '10.0.0.0/24'
  }
}

resource networkInterface
'Microsoft.Network/networkInterfaces@2021-03-01' = {
  name: 'myNic'
  location: location
```

```
  properties: {
    ipConfigurations: [
      {
        name: 'ipConfig1'
        properties: {
          privateIPAllocationMethod: 'Dynamic'
          subnet: {
            id: subnet.id
          }
        }
      }
    ]
  }
  dependsOn: [
    subnet
  ]
}

resource vm 'Microsoft.Compute/virtualMachines@2021-03-
01' = {
  name: 'myVM'
  location: location
```

```
properties: {
  hardwareProfile: {
    vmSize: 'Standard_DS1_v2'
  }
  storageProfile: {
    osDisk: {
      createOption: 'FromImage'
    }
    imageReference: {
      publisher: 'Canonical'
      offer: 'UbuntuServer'
      sku: '18.04-LTS'
      version: 'latest'
    }
  }
  osProfile: {
    computerName: 'myVM'
    adminUsername: 'azureuser'
    adminPassword: 'P@ssword1234'
  }
  networkProfile: {
```

```
        networkInterfaces: [
          {
            id: networkInterface.id
          }
        ]
      }
    }
    dependsOn: [
      networkInterface
    ]
}
```

In the above code snippet, I correctly defined the **networkInterface** resource and set up dependencies so that **vm** depends on **networkInterface**, which in turn depends on **subnet**, which depends on **network**. This ensures that resources are created in the correct order.

Summary

I will summarize by saying that in this chapter I explored the advanced capabilities of Bicep in order to improve my Azure deployments. My first step was to become familiar with the conditions feature of Bicep, which enables me to include or exclude resources based on a set of predetermined criteria. By utilizing this dynamic approach, my templates became more adaptable and flexible to accommodate a variety of deployment scenarios. After that, I proceeded to implement loops in Bicep, which allowed me to deploy multiple instances of a resource in an effective manner by iterating over arrays and objects. This capability proved to be especially helpful when it came to scaling applications and managing tasks that were repetitive.

The next thing I did was concentrate on managing dependencies in Bicep. In order to avoid deployment errors, it was necessary to properly manage dependencies in order to guarantee that resources were created in the appropriate order. I was able to resolve issues such as circular dependencies and complex multi-level dependencies by carefully structuring resource relationships. I also learned how to define dependencies by utilizing the dependsOn property. In addition to that, I experimented with using Azure Key Vault to safely manage confidential information and sensitive data. In order to retrieve and make use of secrets in my deployments, I integrated Key Vault with Bicep. This allowed me to avoid hardcoding sensitive information directly into the templates. The centralization of secret management and the control of access through Key Vault both contributed to an increase in the security of my deployments caused by this.

In conclusion, I addressed the issue of error handling and debugging in the Bicep system. Common errors, such as syntax errors, missing parameters, resource conflicts, and dependency problems, were among the errors that I discovered. I was able to effectively debug and fix these errors by utilizing tools such as the Bicep extension and the Azure Resource Manager tools that are available in Visual Studio Code. Validation of templates, handling of missing parameters, resolution of resource conflicts, and proper management of dependencies were all demonstrated through the inclusion of practical examples. In general, this chapter provided me with the knowledge and skills necessary to manage complex Azure deployments by utilizing advanced Bicep features. This enabled me to ensure that infrastructure management was carried out in an efficient, secure, and error-free manner.

CHAPTER 5: MODULARIZING BICEP TEMPLATES

Brief Introduction

The goal of this chapter is to fully explore the idea of Bicep template modularization, which aids in the management and organization of complex deployments. This chapter will begin with an overview of Bicep modules, explaining what they are and why they are necessary for developing reusable and maintainable infrastructure as code. By breaking down large templates into smaller, more manageable modules, I can streamline the development process and improve readability.

Next, I will learn how to build and use modules in Bicep. This entails creating modules in separate files and referencing them from my main template. I will learn how to pass parameters to modules and retrieve outputs, thereby making my templates more adaptable and reusable. Then I will look at module nesting and reusing, which will help me understand how to create hierarchical structures by nesting modules within other modules. This technique enables me to create complex deployments from simple, reusable building blocks, thereby increasing modularity and reducing duplication.

Finally, I will learn how to manage complex deployments using modules. I will learn how to manage dependencies, pass configuration data, and structure my deployment logic effectively. By the end of this chapter, I will have the ability to organize my Bicep templates into well-structured, modular components, making my infrastructure code more scalable and maintainable.

Bicep Modules Overview

What Are Bicep Modules?

Bicep modules are a way to organize and encapsulate your Bicep code into smaller, reusable components. A module is essentially a Bicep file that defines a part of your infrastructure, which can be referenced and reused in other Bicep files. By breaking down large and complex templates into modules, I can improve the maintainability and readability of my infrastructure code. This modular approach allows me to manage complex deployments more efficiently and encourages the reuse of code across different projects and environments.

In a typical scenario, a module might represent a single resource or a group of related resources, such as a virtual network, a storage account, or a web application. Each module can accept parameters and return outputs, making it flexible and adaptable to different deployment needs.

Capabilities of Bicep Modules

Bicep modules offer several powerful capabilities that enhance the way I manage and deploy Azure resources:

Encapsulation

Modules allow me to encapsulate the logic for deploying specific resources or sets of resources. This means I can hide the complexity of resource definitions within a module and expose only the necessary parameters and outputs. This makes my main Bicep templates simpler and easier to understand.

Reusability

By defining modules for commonly used resources or configurations, I can reuse these modules across multiple deployments. This reduces duplication and ensures consistency in my infrastructure code. For example, I can create a module for deploying a storage account and reuse it whenever I need a storage account in different projects.

Parameterization

Modules can accept parameters, allowing me to customize their behavior based on input values. This makes modules highly flexible and adaptable to different scenarios. I can define parameters for properties such as names, locations, and configurations, and pass different values when referencing the module.

Outputs

Modules can return outputs, which can be used in the parent template or passed to other modules. This allows me to chain modules together and build complex infrastructure configurations. For instance, a virtual network module can output the subnet ID, which can then be used as an input parameter for a virtual machine module.

Organization

Using modules helps me organize my infrastructure code into logical components. This improves the maintainability of my templates and makes it easier to manage large-scale deployments. I can structure my modules hierarchically, creating a clear and logical separation between different parts of my infrastructure.

These features, together with Bicep modules, let me create infrastructure as code that is more modular, reusable, and easy to maintain. The development process is simplified and my deployments are made more scalable and manageable with this modular approach.

Creating and using Modules

Defining Modules

To define a module in Bicep, I create a separate Bicep file that encapsulates the logic for deploying specific resources. This file can then be referenced in other Bicep files, allowing me to reuse the module across different deployments.

For this example, we will create a module to deploy a storage account. I will name the module file **storageAccountModule.bicep**. Save the following code in a file named **storageAccountModule.bicep**:

```
param storageAccountName string

param location string = 'eastus'

param storageAccountType string = 'Standard_LRS'


resource storageAccount
'Microsoft.Storage/storageAccounts@2019-04-01' = {

  name: storageAccountName

  location: location

  sku: {

    name: storageAccountType

  }

  kind: 'StorageV2'

  properties: {}

}


output storageAccountNameOutput string =
storageAccount.name
```

Importing and Referencing Modules

To use the module I defined, I will reference it in my main Bicep file. This involves specifying the module file path and passing the necessary parameters. And then, save the following code in a file named **main.bicep**:

```
param location string = 'eastus'


module storageModule './storageAccountModule.bicep' = {
  name: 'storageModuleDeployment'
  params: {
    storageAccountName: 'mystorageaccount'
    location: location
    storageAccountType: 'Standard_LRS'
  }
}


output storageAccountNameOutput string =
storageModule.outputs.storageAccountNameOutput
```

Here, **module storageModule './storageAccountModule.bicep'** declares a module named **storageModule** and references the **storageAccountModule.bicep** file.

Next, I will use the Azure CLI to deploy the main Bicep template, which references the module.

```
# Create a resource group
az group create --name myResourceGroup --location eastus


# Deploy the main Bicep template
```

In this, **module blobContainerModule './blobContainerModule.bicep'** declares a module named **blobContainerModule** and references the **blobContainerModule.bicep** file. And, **params** section passes parameters to the Blob container module, including the output from the storage account module.

Then, I will deploy the updated **main.bicep** template that includes both the storage account and Blob container modules.

```
# Create a resource group

az group create --name myResourceGroup --location eastus


# Deploy the main Bicep template

az deployment group create \

  --resource-group myResourceGroup \

  --template-file main.bicep
```

This deployment will create a storage account and a Blob container using the defined modules. The main Bicep file references and uses the modules, making the deployment modular and reusable.

Nesting and Reusing Modules

Concept of Nesting

To build a hierarchical structure, nesting is used to arrange modules inside other modules. By combining smaller, reusable components, I am able to construct complex infrastructure configurations using this approach. I can make it easier to manage and reuse resources and logic across my project by nesting modules, which encapsulate them into discrete units.

Sample Program: Reusing and Nesting Modules

We will continue using the example of the storage account and Blob container modules. I will show how to nest these modules within a higher-level module to create a complete storage solution.

I will create a new Bicep file named **storageSolutionModule.bicep** that nests the storage account and Blob container modules.

```
param storageAccountName string

param location string = 'eastus'

param storageAccountType string = 'Standard_LRS'

param containerName string = 'mycontainer'


module storageAccountModule
'./storageAccountModule.bicep' = {

  name: 'storageAccountDeployment'

  params: {

    storageAccountName: storageAccountName

    location: location

    storageAccountType: storageAccountType

  }

}


module blobContainerModule './blobContainerModule.bicep'
= {

  name: 'blobContainerDeployment'

  params: {

    storageAccountName:
storageAccountModule.outputs.storageAccountNameOutput
```

```
    containerName: containerName
  }
}

output storageAccountNameOutput string =
storageAccountModule.outputs.storageAccountNameOutput
output blobContainerNameOutput string =
blobContainerModule.outputs.containerNameOutput
```

In this above higher-level module, I:

- Define parameters for the storage account and Blob container.
- Nest the **`storageAccountModule`** and **`blobContainerModule`**.
- Pass parameters and outputs between these modules.
- Output the storage account name and Blob container name.

Then, update the **`main.bicep`** file to use the new **`storageSolutionModule`**.

```
param location string = 'eastus'

module storageSolutionModule
'./storageSolutionModule.bicep' = {
  name: 'storageSolutionDeployment'
  params: {
    storageAccountName: 'mystorageaccount'
    location: location
    storageAccountType: 'Standard_LRS'
    containerName: 'mycontainer'
```

```
  }
}

output storageAccountNameOutput string =
storageSolutionModule.outputs.storageAccountNameOutput

output blobContainerNameOutput string =
storageSolutionModule.outputs.blobContainerNameOutput
```

In the updated **main.bicep** file:

- I reference the **storageSolutionModule** and pass the necessary parameters.
- I output the results from the **storageSolutionModule**.

Deploy the updated **main.bicep** template that uses the nested **storageSolutionModule** as below:

```
# Create a resource group

az group create --name myResourceGroup --location eastus


# Deploy the main Bicep template

az deployment group create \

  --resource-group myResourceGroup \

  --template-file main.bicep
```

This above deployment will create the complete storage solution, including the storage account and Blob container, by nesting and reusing the modules.

Reusing Modules in Other Projects

Modules can be reused across different projects by referencing them in new Bicep files. Given below is how to reuse the **storageSolutionModule** in another project.

I will create a new Bicep file named **newProject.bicep** to use the **storageSolutionModule**.

```
param location string = 'westus'


module storageSolutionModule
'./storageSolutionModule.bicep' = {
  name: 'storageSolutionDeployment'
  params: {
    storageAccountName: 'newstorageaccount'
    location: location
    storageAccountType: 'Standard_GRS'
    containerName: 'newcontainer'
  }
}


output storageAccountNameOutput string =
storageSolutionModule.outputs.storageAccountNameOutput
output blobContainerNameOutput string =
storageSolutionModule.outputs.blobContainerNameOutput
```

In this new project file:

- I reference the **storageSolutionModule** and pass the required parameters for the new project.
- I output the results from the **storageSolutionModule**.

Then, deploy the **newProject.bicep** template using the Azure CLI as below:

```
# Create a resource group for the new project

az group create --name newProjectResourceGroup --location
westus


# Deploy the new project Bicep template

az deployment group create \

  --resource-group newProjectResourceGroup \

  --template-file newProject.bicep
```

By referencing the **storageSolutionModule**, I can reuse the same storage solution in different projects with different parameters, ensuring consistency and reducing duplication.

Managing Complex Deployments with Modules

Conceptual Overview

When managing complex deployments, breaking down the infrastructure into smaller, manageable modules is crucial. This modular approach helps organize the deployment process, making it easier to develop, debug, and maintain the code. By encapsulating related resources and logic into discrete units, I can enhance reusability and simplify the overall structure of my deployment.

Key steps for managing complex deployments include:

- Break down the infrastructure into functional units or components, such as network configurations, storage accounts, compute resources, and security settings.
- Create individual Bicep modules for each functional unit, encapsulating the logic and resources specific to that unit.
- Structure the modules hierarchically, with higher-level modules referencing and combining lower-level modules.
- Use parameters to customize the behavior and configuration of each module, making them flexible and adaptable.
- Clearly define dependencies between modules to ensure resources are created in the correct order.

Sample Program: Organizing and Structuring Modules

In order to show how to structure these modules, we will expand our current project to include a storage solution that includes a virtual machine and a virtual network.

Create a Virtual Network Module

First, I will create a module to define the virtual network (**virtualNetworkModule.bicep)**

```
param vnetName string

param location string

param addressPrefix string = '10.0.0.0/16'

param subnetName string = 'default'

param subnetPrefix string = '10.0.0.0/24'


resource vnet 'Microsoft.Network/virtualNetworks@2021-02-
01' = {

  name: vnetName

  location: location

  properties: {

    addressSpace: {

      addressPrefixes: [addressPrefix]

    }

    subnets: [

      {

        name: subnetName
```

```
        properties: {
          addressPrefix: subnetPrefix
        }
      }
    ]
  }
}

output vnetId string = vnet.id
output subnetId string = vnet.properties.subnets[0].id
```

Create a Virtual Machine Module

Next, I will create a module to define the virtual machine (**virtualMachineModule.bicep)**

```
param vmName string
param location string
param adminUsername string
param adminPassword string
param subnetId string

resource nic 'Microsoft.Network/networkInterfaces@2021-
03-01' = {
  name: '${vmName}-nic'
```

```
  location: location
  properties: {
    ipConfigurations: [
      {
        name: 'ipConfig1'
        properties: {
          privateIPAllocationMethod: 'Dynamic'
          subnet: {
            id: subnetId
          }
        }
      }
    ]
  }
}

resource vm 'Microsoft.Compute/virtualMachines@2021-03-
01' = {
  name: vmName
  location: location
  properties: {
    hardwareProfile: {
```

```
      vmSize: 'Standard_DS1_v2'
    }
    storageProfile: {
      osDisk: {
        createOption: 'FromImage'
      }
      imageReference: {
        publisher: 'Canonical'
        offer: 'UbuntuServer'
        sku: '18.04-LTS'
        version: 'latest'
      }
    }
    osProfile: {
      computerName: vmName
      adminUsername: adminUsername
      adminPassword: adminPassword
    }
    networkProfile: {
      networkInterfaces: [
        {
```

```
          id: nic.id
        }
      ]
    }
  }
}

output vmId string = vm.id
```

Combine Modules in a Higher-Level Module

I will create a higher-level module (**complexDeploymentModule.bicep)** to combine the virtual network and virtual machine modules with our existing storage solution.

```
param storageAccountName string
param storageLocation string = 'eastus'
param storageAccountType string = 'Standard_LRS'
param containerName string = 'mycontainer'
param vnetName string
param vnetLocation string = 'eastus'
param addressPrefix string = '10.0.0.0/16'
param subnetName string = 'default'
param subnetPrefix string = '10.0.0.0/24'
param vmName string
param vmLocation string = 'eastus'
```

```
param adminUsername string

param adminPassword string


module storageSolutionModule
'./storageSolutionModule.bicep' = {

  name: 'storageSolutionDeployment'

  params: {

    storageAccountName: storageAccountName

    location: storageLocation

    storageAccountType: storageAccountType

    containerName: containerName

  }

}


module virtualNetworkModule
'./virtualNetworkModule.bicep' = {

  name: 'vnetDeployment'

  params: {

    vnetName: vnetName

    location: vnetLocation

    addressPrefix: addressPrefix

    subnetName: subnetName
```

```
    subnetPrefix: subnetPrefix
  }
}

module virtualMachineModule
'./virtualMachineModule.bicep' = {
  name: 'vmDeployment'
  params: {
    vmName: vmName
    location: vmLocation
    adminUsername: adminUsername
    adminPassword: adminPassword
    subnetId: virtualNetworkModule.outputs.subnetId
  }
}

output storageAccountNameOutput string =
storageSolutionModule.outputs.storageAccountNameOutput
output blobContainerNameOutput string =
storageSolutionModule.outputs.blobContainerNameOutput
output vnetIdOutput string =
virtualNetworkModule.outputs.vnetId
output vmIdOutput string =
```

```
virtualMachineModule.outputs.vmId
```

Deploy the Higher-Level Module

Finally, I will reference the higher-level module in the main Bicep file (**main.bicep)** and deploy it.

```
param storageAccountName string

param vnetName string

param vmName string

param adminUsername string

param adminPassword string


module complexDeploymentModule
'./complexDeploymentModule.bicep' = {

  name: 'complexDeployment'

  params: {

    storageAccountName: storageAccountName

    vnetName: vnetName

    vmName: vmName

    adminUsername: adminUsername

    adminPassword: adminPassword

  }

}
```

```
output storageAccountNameOutput string =
complexDeploymentModule.outputs.storageAccountNameOutput

output blobContainerNameOutput string =
complexDeploymentModule.outputs.blobContainerNameOutput

output vnetIdOutput string =
complexDeploymentModule.outputs.vnetIdOutput

output vmIdOutput string =
complexDeploymentModule.outputs.vmIdOutput
```

Deploy the main Bicep file

```
# Create a resource group

az group create --name myResourceGroup --location eastus


# Deploy the main Bicep template

az deployment group create \

  --resource-group myResourceGroup \

  --template-file main.bicep \

  --parameters storageAccountName='mystorageaccount' \

                vnetName='myVnet' \

                vmName='myVM' \

                adminUsername='azureuser' \

                adminPassword='P@ssword1234'
```

Overall, the key to effectively managing complex infrastructure setups is to break them down into smaller modules and arrange them hierarchically. This allows me to handle deployments with greater ease. In order to facilitate scalable and resilient Azure deployments, this method improves the clarity, reusability, and maintainability of my Bicep templates.

Summary

To summarize, I learned how to modularize Bicep templates to better manage complex Azure deployments. I started by learning about Bicep modules and how they turn specific parts of infrastructure into reusable components. This modular approach improves maintainability and readability by breaking up large templates into smaller, more manageable units.

Next, I learned how to create and use modules in Bicep. I was able to reference modules like storage accounts and Blob containers in the main template by creating separate Bicep files for them. This allowed me to pass parameters to the modules and retrieve outputs, making the templates more adaptable and reusable. I saw how to use the Azure CLI to deploy the main Bicep template with referenced modules, resulting in the creation of the resources defined in the modules. I then looked into nesting and reusing modules. By organizing modules hierarchically, I was able to create complex infrastructure configurations from simple, reusable components. I made a higher-level module that combines the storage account and Blob container modules and referenced it in the main Bicep file. This approach enabled me to manage dependencies and pass parameters between nested modules, increasing modularity and reducing duplication.

Finally, I concentrated on managing complex deployments through modules. I learned how to divide the infrastructure into functional units and create separate modules for each one. By structuring these modules hierarchically and using parameters, I was able to customize their behavior and configuration. I illustrated this with a comprehensive example that included storage accounts, virtual networks, and virtual machines, demonstrating how to combine and deploy these components using nested modules. Overall, this chapter taught me how to organize Bicep templates into well-structured, modular components, which improved the scalability, maintainability, and reuse of my Azure deployments.

Chapter 6: Managing Parameters and Variables

Brief Introduction

A detailed understanding and putting into practice the working of more complex methods for controlling Bicep template variables and parameters is the focus of this chapter. This chapter aims to improve my understanding of how to configure parameters and variables to create flexible, dynamic, and secure infrastructure deployments. I will start with advanced parameter configuration, where I will learn how to define complex parameter properties like default values and constraints. These properties allow me to control the input values and ensure they meet specific criteria, which increases the robustness of my templates.

Next, I will look into using arrays and objects as parameters. This feature enables me to incorporate complex data structures into my templates, increasing their power and adaptability to various deployment scenarios. I will look at how to define these complex parameters and access their values through my templates. Then, I will explore scoped variables and outputs. Scoped variables help me manage the scope and lifecycle of values in my templates, ensuring they are used efficiently and effectively. Outputs allow me to retrieve values from deployments that can be used for additional automation or as inputs into other templates.

Finally, I will learn how to pass parameters securely. I will learn how to securely store sensitive information, such as passwords and API keys, within my templates. This includes integrating Azure Key Vault and other techniques to protect sensitive data during the deployment process. By the end of this chapter, I will have a thorough understanding of how to manage parameters and variables in Bicep, allowing me to create more adaptable, dynamic, and secure infrastructure templates for Azure deployments.

Advanced Parameter Configuration

Complex Parameter Types

In Bicep, I can define various complex parameter types to handle different data structures and enhance the flexibility of my templates. These types include strings, integers, booleans, arrays, and objects.

String

Used to store text values.

```
param storageAccountName string
```

Integer

Used to store numeric values.

```
param instanceCount int
```

Boolean

Used to store true/false values.

```
param enableDiagnostics bool
```

Array

Used to store a collection of values.

```
param subnetNames array
```

Object

Used to store a collection of key-value pairs.

```
param vmConfig object
```

In addition to defining parameter types, I can configure advanced properties such as default values, allowed values, and constraints.

Advanced Parameter Properties

Default Values

I can specify a default value for a parameter, which will be used if no value is provided during deployment.

```
param location string = 'eastus'
```

Allowed Values

I can restrict a parameter to a predefined set of allowed values.

```
param storageAccountType string = 'Standard_LRS' {

  allowed: [

    'Standard_LRS'

    'Standard_GRS'
```

```
    'Standard_ZRS'
    'Premium_LRS'
  ]
}
```

Metadata

I can add metadata to provide additional information about a parameter.

```
param instanceCount int {
  metadata: {
    description: 'The number of VM instances to create'
  }
}
```

Advanced Configuration using Parameter Files

Parameter files allow me to define parameter values separately from the Bicep template, making it easier to manage and reuse configurations across different environments.

Create a Parameter File

I will create a JSON parameter file named **azuredeploy.parameters.json** to store the parameter values.

```
{
  "$schema":
"https://schema.management.azure.com/schemas/2019-04-01/deploymentParameters.json#",
  "contentVersion": "1.0.0.0",
  "parameters": {
```

```
"storageAccountName": {
  "value": "mystorageaccount"
},
"location": {
  "value": "westus"
},
"storageAccountType": {
  "value": "Standard_GRS"
},
"subnetNames": {
  "value": [
    "subnet1",
    "subnet2",
    "subnet3"
  ]
},
"vmConfig": {
  "value": {
    "vmSize": "Standard_DS1_v2",
    "adminUsername": "azureuser",
    "adminPassword": "P@ssword1234"
```

```
        }
      }
    }
}
```

Reference Parameter File in Bicep Template

I will define parameters in the Bicep template (**main.bicep**) to match the structure of the parameter file.

```
param storageAccountName string
param location string = 'eastus'
param storageAccountType string = 'Standard_LRS' {
  allowed: [
    'Standard_LRS'
    'Standard_GRS'
    'Standard_ZRS'
    'Premium_LRS'
  ]
}
param subnetNames array
param vmConfig object

resource storageAccount
'Microsoft.Storage/storageAccounts@2019-04-01' = {
```

```
  name: storageAccountName
  location: location
  sku: {
    name: storageAccountType
  }
  kind: 'StorageV2'
  properties: {}
}

resource vnet 'Microsoft.Network/virtualNetworks@2021-02-
01' = {
  name: 'myVnet'
  location: location
  properties: {
    addressSpace: {
      addressPrefixes: [
        '10.0.0.0/16'
      ]
    }
    subnets: [for subnetName in subnetNames: {
      name: subnetName
      properties: {
```

```
        addressPrefix: '10.0.0.0/24'
      }
    }]
  }
}

resource vm 'Microsoft.Compute/virtualMachines@2021-03-
01' = {
  name: 'myVM'
  location: location
  properties: {
    hardwareProfile: {
      vmSize: vmConfig.vmSize
    }
    storageProfile: {
      osDisk: {
        createOption: 'FromImage'
      }
      imageReference: {
        publisher: 'Canonical'
        offer: 'UbuntuServer'
        sku: '18.04-LTS'
```

```
        version: 'latest'
      }
    }
    osProfile: {
      computerName: 'myVM'
      adminUsername: vmConfig.adminUsername
      adminPassword: vmConfig.adminPassword
    }
    networkProfile: {
      networkInterfaces: [
        {
          id: '/subscriptions/<subscription-
id>/resourceGroups/myResourceGroup/providers/Microsoft.Ne
twork/networkInterfaces/myNic'
        }
      ]
    }
  }
}
```

Deploy Bicep Template using Parameter File

```
# Create a resource group
az group create --name myResourceGroup --location eastus
```

```
# Deploy the Bicep template with the parameter file

az deployment group create \

  --resource-group myResourceGroup \

  --template-file main.bicep \

  --parameters @azuredeploy.parameters.json
```

Using parameter files and defining complex parameter types, I can make Bicep templates that are easy to modify and reuse. I am able to more effectively manage infrastructure deployments and adapt to different scenarios with this advanced configuration capability.

Default Values and Constraints

Setting Default Values

In Bicep, I can set default values for parameters to provide predefined values that will be used if no explicit value is provided during deployment. This ensures that my templates have sensible defaults, reducing the need for specifying values for every deployment.

Consider the following example of setting default values:

```
param location string = 'eastus'

param storageAccountType string = 'Standard_LRS'

param enableDiagnostics bool = true
```

Here we set the,

- **`location`**: Default value is 'eastus'.
- **`storageAccountType`**: Default value is 'Standard_LRS'.
- **`enableDiagnostics`**: Default value is **`true`**.

Defining Constraints and Validation

Constraints and validation in Bicep help ensure that the parameters provided during deployment meet specific criteria. This includes setting allowed values, ranges, and metadata descriptions:

- **Allowed Values**: Restricting parameter values to a predefined set of allowed values.
- **Minimum and Maximum Lengths**: Defining constraints on the length of string parameters.
- **Metadata**: Adding descriptions to parameters for better understanding.

Sample Program: Defining Constraints and Validation

We can improve our project by making sure our parameters are validated and by adding constraints as shown below:

```
param location string = 'eastus' {

  allowed: [

    'eastus'

    'westus'

    'centralus'

  ]

  metadata: {

    description: 'The location for all resources'

  }

}


param storageAccountName string {

  metadata: {

    description: 'The name of the storage account'

  }
```

```
}

param storageAccountType string = 'Standard_LRS' {
  allowed: [
    'Standard_LRS'
    'Standard_GRS'
    'Standard_ZRS'
    'Premium_LRS'
  ]
  metadata: {
    description: 'The SKU of the storage account'
  }
}

param subnetNames array = [
  'subnet1'
  'subnet2'
  'subnet3'
]

param vmConfig object {
```

```
  metadata: {
    description: 'Configuration for the virtual machine'
  }
  required: true
}

resource storageAccount
'Microsoft.Storage/storageAccounts@2019-04-01' = {
  name: storageAccountName
  location: location
  sku: {
    name: storageAccountType
  }
  kind: 'StorageV2'
  properties: {}
}

resource vnet 'Microsoft.Network/virtualNetworks@2021-02-
01' = {
  name: 'myVnet'
  location: location
  properties: {
```

```
    addressSpace: {
      addressPrefixes: [
        '10.0.0.0/16'
      ]
    }
    subnets: [for subnetName in subnetNames: {
      name: subnetName
      properties: {
        addressPrefix: '10.0.0.0/24'
      }
    }]
  }
}

resource vm 'Microsoft.Compute/virtualMachines@2021-03-
01' = {
  name: 'myVM'
  location: location
  properties: {
    hardwareProfile: {
      vmSize: vmConfig.vmSize
    }
```

```
    storageProfile: {
      osDisk: {
        createOption: 'FromImage'
      }
      imageReference: {
        publisher: 'Canonical'
        offer: 'UbuntuServer'
        sku: '18.04-LTS'
        version: 'latest'
      }
    }
    osProfile: {
      computerName: 'myVM'
      adminUsername: vmConfig.adminUsername
      adminPassword: vmConfig.adminPassword
    }
    networkProfile: {
      networkInterfaces: [
        {
          id: '/subscriptions/<subscription-
id>/resourceGroups/myResourceGroup/providers/Microsoft.Ne
twork/networkInterfaces/myNic'
```

```
        }
      ]
    }
  }
}
```

In the above script,

- **Location Parameter**: The **`location`** parameter is restricted to the allowed values of 'eastus', 'westus', and 'centralus'. The **`metadata`** field provides a description.
- **Storage Account Name Parameter**: The **`storageAccountName`** parameter includes a description.
- **Storage Account Type Parameter**: The **`storageAccountType`** parameter has allowed values and a description.
- **Subnet Names Parameter**: The **`subnetNames`** parameter is an array with a default value.
- **VM Configuration Parameter**: The **`vmConfig`** parameter is an object with required properties, ensuring that all necessary configuration details are provided.

Create a Parameter File with Constraints

Consider the example of **`azuredeploy.parameters.json`**

```
{
  "$schema":
"https://schema.management.azure.com/schemas/2019-04-01/deploymentParameters.json#",
  "contentVersion": "1.0.0.0",
  "parameters": {
    "location": {
      "value": "westus"
```

```
},
"storageAccountName": {
  "value": "mystorageaccount"
},
"storageAccountType": {
  "value": "Standard_GRS"
},
"subnetNames": {
  "value": [
    "subnetA",
    "subnetB",
    "subnetC"
  ]
},
"vmConfig": {
  "value": {
    "vmSize": "Standard_DS1_v2",
    "adminUsername": "azureuser",
    "adminPassword": "P@ssword1234"
  }
}
```

```
  }
}
```

And, this deployment will use the defined parameters, default values, and constraints to create the resources. The constraints ensure that the provided values meet the required criteria, preventing deployment errors and ensuring consistent configurations.

Using Arrays and Objects in Parameters

Introduction to Arrays and Objects in Parameters

In Bicep, arrays and objects enable me to pass complex data structures into my templates, providing flexibility and enhancing the ability to handle dynamic configurations. Arrays allow me to group multiple values together, while objects allow me to create key-value pairs for more structured data.

Arrays

Used to store a collection of values.

```
param subnetNames array = [
  'subnet1'
  'subnet2'
  'subnet3'
]
```

Objects

Used to store a collection of key-value pairs.

```
param vmConfig object = {
  vmSize: 'Standard_DS1_v2'
```

```
  adminUsername: 'azureuser'

  adminPassword: 'P@ssword1234'

}
```

Sample Program: Use of Arrays and Objects

We will define subnets using an array and configure a virtual machine using an object as shown below.

```
param location string = 'eastus' {

  allowed: [

    'eastus'

    'westus'

    'centralus'

  ]

  metadata: {

    description: 'The location for all resources'

  }

}


param storageAccountName string {

  metadata: {

    description: 'The name of the storage account'

  }

}
```

```
param storageAccountType string = 'Standard_LRS' {
  allowed: [
    'Standard_LRS'
    'Standard_GRS'
    'Standard_ZRS'
    'Premium_LRS'
  ]
  metadata: {
    description: 'The SKU of the storage account'
  }
}

param subnetNames array = [
  'subnet1'
  'subnet2'
  'subnet3'
] {
  metadata: {
    description: 'List of subnet names'
  }
```

```
}

param vmConfig object {
  metadata: {
    description: 'Configuration for the virtual machine'
  }
  required: true
}

resource storageAccount
'Microsoft.Storage/storageAccounts@2019-04-01' = {
  name: storageAccountName
  location: location
  sku: {
    name: storageAccountType
  }
  kind: 'StorageV2'
  properties: {}
}

resource vnet 'Microsoft.Network/virtualNetworks@2021-02-
01' = {
```

```
  name: 'myVnet'
  location: location
  properties: {
    addressSpace: {
      addressPrefixes: [
        '10.0.0.0/16'
      ]
    }
    subnets: [for subnetName in subnetNames: {
      name: subnetName
      properties: {
        addressPrefix: '10.0.0.0/24'
      }
    }]
  }
}

resource nic 'Microsoft.Network/networkInterfaces@2021-
03-01' = {
  name: 'myNic'
  location: location
  properties: {
```

```
    ipConfigurations: [
      {
        name: 'ipConfig1'
        properties: {
          privateIPAllocationMethod: 'Dynamic'
          subnet: {
            id:
resourceId('Microsoft.Network/virtualNetworks/subnets',
'myVnet', 'subnet1')
          }
        }
      }
    ]
  }
}

resource vm 'Microsoft.Compute/virtualMachines@2021-03-
01' = {
  name: 'myVM'
  location: location
  properties: {
    hardwareProfile: {
```

```
    vmSize: vmConfig.vmSize
  }
  storageProfile: {
    osDisk: {
      createOption: 'FromImage'
    }
    imageReference: {
      publisher: 'Canonical'
      offer: 'UbuntuServer'
      sku: '18.04-LTS'
      version: 'latest'
    }
  }
  osProfile: {
    computerName: 'myVM'
    adminUsername: vmConfig.adminUsername
    adminPassword: vmConfig.adminPassword
  }
  networkProfile: {
    networkInterfaces: [
      {
```

```
          id: nic.id
        }
      ]
    }
  }
}
```

Here in the above example,

- **subnetNames** array parameter holds a list of subnet names. I use a **for** loop to iterate over the array and create subnets dynamically within the virtual network resource.
- **vmConfig** object parameter holds the virtual machine configuration, including the VM size, admin username, and admin password. I reference these properties within the virtual machine resource.

Following is the parameter file **(azuredeploy.parameters.json)** with arrays and objects:

```
{
  "$schema":
"https://schema.management.azure.com/schemas/2019-04-01/deploymentParameters.json#",
  "contentVersion": "1.0.0.0",
  "parameters": {
    "location": {
      "value": "westus"
    },
    "storageAccountName": {
      "value": "mystorageaccount"
```

```
    },
    "storageAccountType": {
      "value": "Standard_GRS"
    },
    "subnetNames": {
      "value": [
        "subnetA",
        "subnetB",
        "subnetC"
      ]
    },
    "vmConfig": {
      "value": {
        "vmSize": "Standard_DS1_v2",
        "adminUsername": "azureuser",
        "adminPassword": "P@ssword1234"
      }
    }
  }
}
```

Now, deploy the template with arrays and objects:

```
# Create a resource group

az group create --name myResourceGroup --location eastus


# Deploy the Bicep template with the parameter file

az deployment group create \

  --resource-group myResourceGroup \

  --template-file main.bicep \

  --parameters @azuredeploy.parameters.json
```

You will get a storage account, a virtual network with multiple subnets, an interface for the network, and a virtual machine with the parameters you provided when you deploy this. The use of arrays and objects in the parameters allows me to handle more intricate and dynamic configurations, which in turn makes my templates exceptionally versatile and powerful.

Scoped Variables and Outputs

The scope of a template is the extent to which its variables and outputs are visible and how long they remain visible. If you want to manage data access and usage across different parts of a deployment, you must understand scope. To make sure my templates have good data encapsulation and flow, I use scoped variables and outputs so I can control their definition and usage context.

Scoped Variables and Outputs

Scoped variables in Bicep are variables whose visibility is limited to a specific context, such as within a module or a loop. This ensures that variables are only accessible where they are needed, reducing the risk of conflicts and making the template easier to understand and maintain.

Scoped outputs allow me to return values from a specific scope, such as a module, to the parent template. This enables the parent template to access and use values generated within a module, facilitating data flow between different parts of the deployment.

Sample Program: Scoped Variables and Outputs

To demonstrate the use of scoped variables and outputs, we will create a module for network resources and use scoped variables and outputs within our continued example.

```
param location string

param subnetNames array


var addressPrefix = '10.0.0.0/16'


resource vnet 'Microsoft.Network/virtualNetworks@2021-02-01' = {

  name: 'myVnet'

  location: location

  properties: {

    addressSpace: {

      addressPrefixes: [

        addressPrefix

      ]

    }

    subnets: [for subnetName in subnetNames: {

      name: subnetName

      properties: {

        addressPrefix: '10.0.0.0/24'

      }

    }]
```

```
  }
}

output vnetId string = vnet.id
output subnetIds array = [for subnet in
vnet.properties.subnets: subnet.id]
```

In the above module:

- I define a scoped variable **`addressPrefix`** for the virtual network's address space.
- I create a virtual network resource with dynamically created subnets using the **`subnetNames`** parameter.
- I define outputs to return the virtual network ID and the IDs of the created subnets.

Next, we reference the network module in the main bicep file.

```
param location string = 'eastus' {
  allowed: [
    'eastus'
    'westus'
    'centralus'
  ]
  metadata: {
    description: 'The location for all resources'
  }
}
```

```
param storageAccountName string {
  metadata: {
    description: 'The name of the storage account'
  }
}

param storageAccountType string = 'Standard_LRS' {
  allowed: [
    'Standard_LRS'
    'Standard_GRS'
    'Standard_ZRS'
    'Premium_LRS'
  ]
  metadata: {
    description: 'The SKU of the storage account'
  }
}

param subnetNames array = [
  'subnet1'
  'subnet2'
```

```
  'subnet3'
] {
  metadata: {
    description: 'List of subnet names'
  }
}

param vmConfig object {
  metadata: {
    description: 'Configuration for the virtual machine'
  }
  required: true
}

module networkModule './networkModule.bicep' = {
  name: 'networkDeployment'
  params: {
    location: location
    subnetNames: subnetNames
  }
}
```

```
resource storageAccount
'Microsoft.Storage/storageAccounts@2019-04-01' = {

  name: storageAccountName

  location: location

  sku: {

    name: storageAccountType

  }

  kind: 'StorageV2'

  properties: {}

}


resource nic 'Microsoft.Network/networkInterfaces@2021-
03-01' = {

  name: 'myNic'

  location: location

  properties: {

    ipConfigurations: [

      {

        name: 'ipConfig1'

        properties: {

          privateIPAllocationMethod: 'Dynamic'
```

```
          subnet: {
            id: networkModule.outputs.subnetIds[0]
          }
        }
      }
    ]
  }
}

resource vm 'Microsoft.Compute/virtualMachines@2021-03-01' = {
  name: 'myVM'
  location: location
  properties: {
    hardwareProfile: {
      vmSize: vmConfig.vmSize
    }
    storageProfile: {
      osDisk: {
        createOption: 'FromImage'
      }
      imageReference: {
```

```
        publisher: 'Canonical'
        offer: 'UbuntuServer'
        sku: '18.04-LTS'
        version: 'latest'
      }
    }
    osProfile: {
      computerName: 'myVM'
      adminUsername: vmConfig.adminUsername
      adminPassword: vmConfig.adminPassword
    }
    networkProfile: {
      networkInterfaces: [
        {
          id: nic.id
        }
      ]
    }
  }
}
```

```
output vnetIdOutput string = networkModule.outputs.vnetId

output subnetIdsOutput array =
networkModule.outputs.subnetIds
```

In this main Bicep file:

- I reference the **networkModule** and pass the required parameters.
- I use the scoped outputs from the **networkModule** to configure the network interface (**nic**) and virtual machine (**vm**).
- I define outputs in the main Bicep file to return the virtual network ID and subnet IDs from the **networkModule**.

Now we move to parameter the file with arrays and objects:

```
{

  "$schema":
"https://schema.management.azure.com/schemas/2019-04-
01/deploymentParameters.json#",

  "contentVersion": "1.0.0.0",

  "parameters": {

    "location": {

      "value": "westus"

    },

    "storageAccountName": {

      "value": "mystorageaccount"

    },

    "storageAccountType": {

      "value": "Standard_GRS"
```

```
    },
    "subnetNames": {
      "value": [
        "subnetA",
        "subnetB",
        "subnetC"
      ]
    },
    "vmConfig": {
      "value": {
        "vmSize": "Standard_DS1_v2",
        "adminUsername": "azureuser",
        "adminPassword": "P@ssword1234"
      }
    }
  }
}
```

Then finally, we deploy the template with scoped variables and outputs.

```
# Create a resource group
az group create --name myResourceGroup --location eastus
```

```
# Deploy the Bicep template with the parameter file

az deployment group create \

  --resource-group myResourceGroup \

  --template-file main.bicep \

  --parameters @azuredeploy.parameters.json
```

This deployment will create a storage account, a virtual network with multiple subnets, a network interface, and a virtual machine. The use of scoped variables and outputs ensures that the virtual network ID and subnet IDs are correctly passed between the modules and the main template, maintaining proper encapsulation and data flow.

Passing Parameters Securely

When dealing with sensitive data such as passwords, API keys, or connection strings, it is crucial to handle and pass these parameters securely. Hardcoding sensitive information directly in the Bicep templates or parameter files is not secure. Instead, I can use Azure Key Vault to securely store and manage sensitive information and reference these secrets within my Bicep templates. Azure Key Vault provides a centralized, secure storage for secrets, allowing me to access them safely during deployments. We can store secrets in Azure Key Vault and then use them in our Bicep templates to pass parameters securely.

Following is the process:

Setup Azure Key Vault

First, I will create an Azure Key Vault and store a secret in it.

```
# Create a resource group for the Key Vault

az group create --name myKeyVaultResourceGroup --location
eastus



# Create the Key Vault

az keyvault create --name myKeyVault --resource-group
```

```
myKeyVaultResourceGroup --location eastus


# Store a secret in the Key Vault

az keyvault secret set --vault-name myKeyVault --name
mySecret --value "P@ssword1234"
```

Reference Azure Key Vault Secrets

Next, I will update my Bicep template to retrieve the secret from Azure Key Vault and use it as a parameter.

```
param location string = 'eastus' {

  allowed: [

    'eastus'

    'westus'

    'centralus'

  ]

  metadata: {

    description: 'The location for all resources'

  }

}


param storageAccountName string {

  metadata: {

    description: 'The name of the storage account'
```

```
  }
}

param storageAccountType string = 'Standard_LRS' {
  allowed: [
    'Standard_LRS'
    'Standard_GRS'
    'Standard_ZRS'
    'Premium_LRS'
  ]
  metadata: {
    description: 'The SKU of the storage account'
  }
}

param subnetNames array = [
  'subnet1'
  'subnet2'
  'subnet3'
] {
  metadata: {
```

```
    description: 'List of subnet names'
  }
}

param adminUsername string = 'azureuser'

@secure()
param adminPassword string

module networkModule './networkModule.bicep' = {
  name: 'networkDeployment'
  params: {
    location: location
    subnetNames: subnetNames
  }
}

resource storageAccount
'Microsoft.Storage/storageAccounts@2019-04-01' = {
  name: storageAccountName
  location: location
  sku: {
```

```
    name: storageAccountType
  }
  kind: 'StorageV2'
  properties: {}
}

resource nic 'Microsoft.Network/networkInterfaces@2021-
03-01' = {
  name: 'myNic'
  location: location
  properties: {
    ipConfigurations: [
      {
        name: 'ipConfig1'
        properties: {
          privateIPAllocationMethod: 'Dynamic'
          subnet: {
            id: networkModule.outputs.subnetIds[0]
          }
        }
      }
    ]
```

```
  }
}

resource vm 'Microsoft.Compute/virtualMachines@2021-03-
01' = {
  name: 'myVM'
  location: location
  properties: {
    hardwareProfile: {
      vmSize: 'Standard_DS1_v2'
    }
    storageProfile: {
      osDisk: {
        createOption: 'FromImage'
      }
      imageReference: {
        publisher: 'Canonical'
        offer: 'UbuntuServer'
        sku: '18.04-LTS'
        version: 'latest'
      }
    }
```

```
    osProfile: {
      computerName: 'myVM'
      adminUsername: adminUsername
      adminPassword: adminPassword
    }
    networkProfile: {
      networkInterfaces: [
        {
          id: nic.id
        }
      ]
    }
  }
}

output vnetIdOutput string = networkModule.outputs.vnetId
output subnetIdsOutput array =
networkModule.outputs.subnetIds
```

In this updated **`main.bicep`** file:

- I define a secure parameter **`adminPassword`** using the **`@secure()`** decorator.
- The **`adminPassword`** parameter will be populated with the secret value from Azure Key Vault.

Create Parameter File Referencing the Key Vault Secret

Now, I will create a parameter file that references the secret stored in Azure Key Vault.

```
{
  "$schema":
"https://schema.management.azure.com/schemas/2019-04-01/deploymentParameters.json#",
  "contentVersion": "1.0.0.0",
  "parameters": {
    "location": {
      "value": "westus"
    },
    "storageAccountName": {
      "value": "mystorageaccount"
    },
    "storageAccountType": {
      "value": "Standard_GRS"
    },
    "subnetNames": {
      "value": [
        "subnetA",
        "subnetB",
        "subnetC"
```

```
        ]
      },
      "adminPassword": {
        "reference": {
          "keyVault": {
            "id": "/subscriptions/<subscription-id>/resourceGroups/myKeyVaultResourceGroup/providers/Microsoft.KeyVault/vaults/myKeyVault"
          },
          "secretName": "mySecret"
        }
      }
    }
}
```

In the above parameter file, the **adminPassword** parameter uses a **reference** object to retrieve the secret from Azure Key Vault. And don't forget to replace **<subscription-id>** with your actual Azure subscription ID.

Deploy the Template with Secure Parameters

```
# Create a resource group for the deployment
az group create --name myResourceGroup --location eastus


# Deploy the Bicep template with the parameter file
az deployment group create \
```

```
--resource-group myResourceGroup \
--template-file main.bicep \
--parameters @azuredeploy.parameters.json
```

This deployment securely retrieves the **adminPassword** from Azure Key Vault and uses it in the deployment without exposing the sensitive value in the template or parameter files. My Bicep templates can safely handle and pass sensitive parameters thanks to Azure Key Vault. This method strengthens the safety of my deployments because it consolidates secret management and safeguards sensitive data all through the deployment procedure.

Summary

In sum, I picked up some knowledge on how to use Bicep templates' parameter and variable management features to build infrastructure deployments that are adaptable, dynamic, and secure. I began by exploring advanced parameter configurations, such as setting default values, specifying constraints, and adding metadata. This enabled me to control input values and ensure they meet specific criteria, thereby increasing the robustness of my templates. I then experimented with using arrays and objects as parameters, allowing me to handle complex data structures. Passing arrays allowed me to group multiple values together, while objects allowed me to create key-value pairs for more structured data. I practiced implementing these in my project, allowing for dynamic subnet and virtual machine configurations.

Next, I looked at scoped variables and outputs, learning how to control the visibility and lifecycle of variables across different parts of a deployment. Scoped variables ensured that data was only available when needed, reducing conflicts and improving maintainability. Scoped outputs enabled me to return values from modules to the parent template, which improved data flow and modularity. Finally, I focused on securely passing parameters through Azure Key Vault. I created a Key Vault, stored secrets, and referenced them in my Bicep templates. This method ensured that sensitive information, such as passwords, was kept secure and not exposed in the template or parameter files. By integrating Azure Key Vault, I centralized secret management and safeguarded sensitive data during deployment.

Overall, Chapter 6 provided me with advanced skills for effectively managing parameters and variables in Bicep, which improved the flexibility, security, and maintainability of my Azure infrastructure deployment.

CHAPTER 7: INTEGRATION AND DEPLOYMENT STRATEGIES

Brief Introduction

In this chapter, I will look at integration and deployment options for increasing the automation and stability of my Bicep-based infrastructure deployments. This chapter will provide a thorough overview of how to implement Bicep templates into Continuous Integration/Continuous Deployment (CI/CD) pipelines, allowing for efficient and consistent deployments.

I will start by learning how to connect Bicep with CI/CD pipelines, with a focus on automating deployment and ensuring that my infrastructure is updated seamlessly. This will feature real examples of leveraging GitHub Actions and Azure DevOps for Bicep deployments, as well as how to create pipelines that automatically validate and deploy Bicep templates. Next, I will go over deploying to several environments, including development, staging, and production. I will learn how to handle environment-specific configurations and ensure consistency across several environments. This section will also go over rollback and rollforward procedures, including how to manage deployment problems and revert to stable states before moving on to newer versions. I will also learn about monitoring and auditing deployments, as well as how to track changes and verify compliance with company policies. This includes implementing logging and alerting tools to monitor the status of my deployments. Furthermore, I plan to explore blue-green deployments, an approach for minimizing downtime and reducing risks during updates.

Finally, I will go over automated testing of Bicep templates to ensure that my infrastructure as code is stable and error-free before deployment. By the end of this chapter, I will have the knowledge and tools to efficiently integrate Bicep into modern deployment procedures, resulting in strong, automated, and secure infrastructure management.

Integrating Bicep with CI/CD Pipelines

Essentials of CI/CD

Continuous Integration (CI) and Continuous Deployment (CD) are essential practices in modern software development and DevOps. CI involves automatically integrating code changes from multiple contributors into a shared repository, where automated builds and tests are run to detect integration issues early. CD extends this by automatically deploying the integrated and tested code to various environments, ensuring that the software is always in a deployable state.

CI/CD pipelines streamline the development process by automating repetitive tasks, reducing human error, and enabling faster delivery of high-quality software. The key components of a CI/CD pipeline include:

- **Source Code Repository**: Where the codebase is stored and managed, e.g., GitHub.
- **Build System**: Compiles the code and runs automated tests.
- **Deployment System**: Deploys the tested code to target environments.

- **Monitoring and Alerts**: Tracks the deployment status and alerts on issues.

Introduction to Azure DevOps

Azure DevOps is a suite of development tools provided by Microsoft for planning, developing, testing, and delivering software. It offers a comprehensive set of features for CI/CD, including:

- **Azure Repos**: Source code management with Git repositories.
- **Azure Pipelines**: CI/CD pipelines for building, testing, and deploying code.
- **Azure Boards**: Agile planning and project management tools.
- **Azure Artifacts**: Package management for artifacts.
- **Azure Test Plans**: Tools for automated and manual testing.

Using Azure DevOps, I can create robust CI/CD pipelines that integrate with various tools and services, including GitHub, to automate the deployment of Bicep templates.

Setting up CI/CD Pipeline

We will set up a CI/CD pipeline to automate the deployment of a Bicep template using GitHub Actions and Azure DevOps.

Setup the Project Repository

First, I will create a GitHub repository to store the Bicep templates and pipeline configurations.

```
# Create a new GitHub repository

gh repo create my-bicep-project --public --confirm



# Clone the repository locally

git clone https://github.com/<your-username>/my-bicep-
project.git

cd my-bicep-project
```

Create a Bicep template file **`(main.bicep)`** in the repository.

```
param location string = 'eastus'
```

```
param storageAccountName string

param storageAccountType string = 'Standard_LRS'


resource storageAccount
'Microsoft.Storage/storageAccounts@2019-04-01' = {

  name: storageAccountName

  location: location

  sku: {

    name: storageAccountType

  }

  kind: 'StorageV2'

  properties: {}

}
```

Commit and Push the Changes

```
# Add the Bicep template to the repository

git add main.bicep

git commit -m "Add Bicep template"

git push origin main
```

Setup GitHub Actions

GitHub Actions provides a way to automate workflows directly within the GitHub repository. I will create a workflow to validate and deploy the Bicep template using Azure CLI.

Create a workflow file (**`.github/workflows/deploy.yml`**) in the repository.

```
name: Deploy Bicep Template

on:
  push:
    branches:
      - main

jobs:
  build:
    runs-on: ubuntu-latest

    steps:
      - name: Checkout repository
        uses: actions/checkout@v2

      - name: Set up Azure CLI
        uses: azure/cli@v1

      - name: Log in to Azure
        uses: azure/login@v1
        with:
```

```
        creds: ${{ secrets.AZURE_CREDENTIALS }}

    - name: Deploy Bicep template
      run: |
        az group create --name myResourceGroup --
location eastus
        az deployment group create \
          --resource-group myResourceGroup \
          --template-file main.bicep \
          --parameters
storageAccountName=myStorageAccount
```

In this workflow:

- The **on** block specifies that the workflow runs on pushes to the **main** branch.
- The **jobs** block defines a **build** job that runs on an Ubuntu runner.
- The steps include checking out the repository, setting up Azure CLI, logging into Azure using credentials stored in GitHub Secrets, and deploying the Bicep template using Azure CLI commands.

In the GitHub repository, navigate to **Settings** > **Secrets** > **New repository secret** and add the Azure credentials as a secret named **AZURE_CREDENTIALS**. The credentials can be obtained by creating a service principal in Azure.

```
# Create a service principal and output the credentials
az ad sp create-for-rbac --name "myServicePrincipal" --
sdk-auth
```

Copy the JSON output and paste it into the **Value** field of the new GitHub secret.

Setup Azure DevOps Pipeline

Azure DevOps Pipelines provide another robust CI/CD solution for deploying Bicep templates. Here, I will create a pipeline to automate the deployment process.

- Go to Azure DevOps and create a new project.
- Navigate to **`Pipelines`** > **`Create Pipeline`**.
- Connect to the GitHub repository containing the Bicep templates.
- Select the repository and configure the pipeline using the YAML file.

Create a pipeline YAML file **`(azure-pipelines.yml)`** in the repository.

```
trigger:

- main


pool:

  vmImage: 'ubuntu-latest'


steps:

- checkout: self


- task: AzureCLI@2

  inputs:

    azureSubscription: 'MyAzureSubscription'

    scriptType: 'bash'

    scriptLocation: 'inlineScript'

    inlineScript: |
```

```
az group create --name myResourceGroup --location
eastus

    az deployment group create \

      --resource-group myResourceGroup \

      --template-file main.bicep \

      --parameters storageAccountName=myStorageAccount

  addSpnToEnvironment: true
```

In this pipeline:

- The **`trigger`** block specifies that the pipeline runs on pushes to the **`main`** branch.
- The **`pool`** block specifies the agent pool to use.
- The **`steps`** block includes tasks to check out the repository and run Azure CLI commands to deploy the Bicep template.

Next, configure service connection as below:

- In the Azure DevOps project, navigate to **`Project settings`** > **`Service connections`**.
- Create a new service connection for Azure Resource Manager.
- Use the service principal credentials to configure the service connection and name it **`MyAzureSubscription`**.

These instructions will show me how to use Azure DevOps and GitHub Actions to connect Bicep templates to continuous integration and continuous delivery pipelines. This automation ensures that my Azure infrastructure is deployed consistently and reliably, as well as managed efficiently.

Automating Bicep Deployments with GitHub Actions

GitHub Actions is a powerful automation tool that allows me to define workflows directly within my GitHub repository. These workflows can automate tasks such as building, testing, and deploying code. By using GitHub Actions, I can create a CI/CD pipeline that automatically deploys Bicep templates whenever changes are pushed to the repository.

We will go through the process of setting up a GitHub Actions workflow to automate the deployment of Bicep templates.

Create a GitHub Repository

First, I will create a GitHub repository to store the Bicep templates and workflow configuration.

```
# Create a new GitHub repository

gh repo create my-bicep-project --public --confirm


# Clone the repository locally

git clone https://github.com/<your-username>/my-bicep-project.git

cd my-bicep-project
```

Create a Bicep template file in the repository.

```
param location string = 'eastus'

param storageAccountName string

param storageAccountType string = 'Standard_LRS'


resource storageAccount
'Microsoft.Storage/storageAccounts@2019-04-01' = {

  name: storageAccountName

  location: location

  sku: {

    name: storageAccountType

  }
```

```
  kind: 'StorageV2'
  properties: {}
}
```

Commit and push the changes.

```
# Add the Bicep template to the repository
git add main.bicep
git commit -m "Add Bicep template"
git push origin main
```

Setup GitHub Actions Workflow

To automate the deployment, I will create a GitHub Actions workflow that uses the Azure CLI to deploy the Bicep template.

First, create a workflow file in the **.github/workflows** directory of the repository.

```
name: Deploy Bicep Template

on:
  push:
    branches:
      - main

jobs:
  deploy:
    runs-on: ubuntu-latest
```

```
    steps:
      - name: Checkout repository
        uses: actions/checkout@v2

      - name: Set up Azure CLI
        uses: azure/cli@v1

      - name: Log in to Azure
        uses: azure/login@v1
        with:
          creds: ${{ secrets.AZURE_CREDENTIALS }}

      - name: Deploy Bicep template
        run: |
          az group create --name myResourceGroup --
location eastus
          az deployment group create \
            --resource-group myResourceGroup \
            --template-file main.bicep \
            --parameters
storageAccountName=myStorageAccount
```

In the above workflow file,

- The workflow triggers on pushes to the **main** branch.
- The **deploy** job runs on an Ubuntu runner and includes steps to:
    - Check out the repository.
    - Set up the Azure CLI.
    - Log in to Azure using credentials stored in GitHub Secrets.
    - Deploy the Bicep template using Azure CLI commands.

To securely log in to Azure, I will add the service principal credentials to GitHub Secrets.

```
# Create a service principal and output the credentials

az ad sp create-for-rbac --name "myServicePrincipal" --
sdk-auth
```

Copy the JSON output and add it as a secret named **AZURE_CREDENTIALS** in the GitHub repository:

1. Navigate to **Settings** > **Secrets** > **New repository secret**.
2. Name the secret **AZURE_CREDENTIALS** and paste the JSON credentials into the **Value** field.

Deploy the Workflow

With the workflow and secrets set up, I will push a change to the **main** branch to trigger the deployment.

```
# Make a small change to trigger the workflow

echo "# Bicep Deployment" >> README.md

git add README.md

git commit -m "Update README"

git push origin main
```

The push to the **main** branch will trigger the GitHub Actions workflow, which will:

1. Check out the repository.

2. Set up the Azure CLI.
3. Log in to Azure using the provided credentials.
4. Create a resource group and deploy the Bicep template to Azure.

I can monitor the progress and results of the workflow by navigating to the **Actions** tab in the GitHub repository. With this, I ensure that infrastructure changes are automatically tested and deployed whenever changes are pushed to the repository.

Deployment to Multiple Environments

When deploying infrastructure, it's crucial to maintain separate environments for development, staging, and production. This ensures that changes can be tested thoroughly before they reach production, minimizing the risk of downtime and other issues.

To deploy environment-specific Bicep templates, I can create separate parameter files for each environment and use GitHub Actions to handle these deployments. We will start by setting up environment-specific parameter files and then configure the GitHub Actions workflow to manage deployments across multiple environments.

Create Parameter Files for Each Environment

First, I will create separate parameter files for development, staging, and production environments.

- Parameter File 1: **parameters.dev.json**

```
{
  "$schema":
"https://schema.management.azure.com/schemas/2019-04-01/deploymentParameters.json#",
  "contentVersion": "1.0.0.0",
  "parameters": {
    "location": {
      "value": "eastus"
    },
```

```
    "storageAccountName": {
      "value": "devstorageaccount"
    },
    "storageAccountType": {
      "value": "Standard_LRS"
    }
  }
}
```

- Parameter File 2: **parameters.staging.json**

```
{
  "$schema":
"https://schema.management.azure.com/schemas/2019-04-01/deploymentParameters.json#",
  "contentVersion": "1.0.0.0",
  "parameters": {
    "location": {
      "value": "westus"
    },
    "storageAccountName": {
      "value": "stagingstorageaccount"
    },
    "storageAccountType": {
```

```
      "value": "Standard_GRS"
    }
  }
}
```

- Parameter File 3: **parameters.prod.json**

```
{
  "$schema":
"https://schema.management.azure.com/schemas/2019-04-
01/deploymentParameters.json#",
  "contentVersion": "1.0.0.0",
  "parameters": {
    "location": {
      "value": "centralus"
    },
    "storageAccountName": {
      "value": "prodstorageaccount"
    },
    "storageAccountType": {
      "value": "Premium_LRS"
    }
  }
}
```

Update GitHub Actions Workflow

Next, I will modify the GitHub Actions workflow to handle deployments to multiple environments based on the branch name.

```
name: Deploy Bicep Template

on:
  push:
    branches:
      - main
      - develop
      - staging

jobs:
  deploy:
    runs-on: ubuntu-latest

    steps:
      - name: Checkout repository
        uses: actions/checkout@v2

      - name: Set up Azure CLI
        uses: azure/cli@v1
```

```
      - name: Log in to Azure
        uses: azure/login@v1
        with:
          creds: ${{ secrets.AZURE_CREDENTIALS }}

      - name: Deploy to development
        if: github.ref == 'refs/heads/develop'
        run: |
          az group create --name myResourceGroup-dev --
location eastus
          az deployment group create \
            --resource-group myResourceGroup-dev \
            --template-file main.bicep \
            --parameters @parameters.dev.json

      - name: Deploy to staging
        if: github.ref == 'refs/heads/staging'
        run: |
          az group create --name myResourceGroup-staging
--location westus
          az deployment group create \
```

```
          --resource-group myResourceGroup-staging \
          --template-file main.bicep \
          --parameters @parameters.staging.json

    - name: Deploy to production
      if: github.ref == 'refs/heads/main'
      run: |
        az group create --name myResourceGroup-prod --
location centralus
        az deployment group create \
          --resource-group myResourceGroup-prod \
          --template-file main.bicep \
          --parameters @parameters.prod.json
```

In this workflow,

- The workflow triggers on pushes to the **`develop`**, **`staging`**, and **`main`** branches.
- The **`deploy`** job includes steps to:
    - Check out the repository.
    - Set up the Azure CLI.
    - Log in to Azure using credentials stored in GitHub Secrets.
    - Deploy the Bicep template to the appropriate environment based on the branch name.

Deploying to Multiple Environments

By pushing changes to different branches, I can trigger environment-specific deployments.

- Deploy to Development

```
# Create a new branch for development
git checkout -b develop


# Make changes to trigger deployment
echo "# Development Deployment" >> README.md
git add README.md
git commit -m "Update README for development"
git push origin develop
```

This push will trigger the workflow, deploying the Bicep template to the development environment using **`parameters.dev.json`**.

- Deploy to Staging

```
# Create a new branch for staging
git checkout -b staging


# Make changes to trigger deployment
echo "# Staging Deployment" >> README.md
git add README.md
git commit -m "Update README for staging"
git push origin staging
```

This push will trigger the workflow, deploying the Bicep template to the staging environment using **`parameters.staging.json`**.

- Deploy to Production

```
# Merge changes to main branch for production
```

```
git checkout main

git merge develop


# Push changes to trigger deployment

git push origin main
```

This push will trigger the workflow, deploying the Bicep template to the production environment using **`parameters.prod.json`**.

The configuration of the GitHub Actions workflow to manage multiple environments and the creation of environment-specific parameter files allow me to guarantee consistent and dependable deployments in development, staging, and production. This method minimizes the possibility of problems and downtime by letting me test modifications extensively prior to their release to production.

Rollback and Rollforward Strategies

When deploying infrastructure, it's essential to have strategies in place to handle failures and ensure that the system remains stable. Rollback and rollforward strategies are two approaches to manage deployment issues:

- **Rollback**: This strategy involves reverting to a previous stable state if the current deployment fails. It ensures that the system can quickly recover from errors by restoring a known good configuration.
- **Rollforward**: This strategy involves deploying a new, corrected version to fix the issues introduced in the failed deployment. Instead of reverting changes, it aims to move forward to a stable state with a new deployment.

Implementing Rollback Strategy

To implement a rollback strategy, I will maintain previous versions of the deployment configurations and revert to a known good state in case of failure. We will set up a GitHub Actions workflow to handle rollbacks for our project.

Setup GitHub Actions Workflow for Rollback

I will modify the GitHub Actions workflow to include rollback steps.

```yaml
name: Deploy Bicep Template

on:
  push:
    branches:
      - main
      - develop
      - staging

jobs:
  deploy:
    runs-on: ubuntu-latest

    steps:
      - name: Checkout repository
        uses: actions/checkout@v2

      - name: Set up Azure CLI
        uses: azure/cli@v1

      - name: Log in to Azure
```

```
        uses: azure/login@v1
        with:
          creds: ${{ secrets.AZURE_CREDENTIALS }}

      - name: Deploy to development
        if: github.ref == 'refs/heads/develop'
        run: |
          az group create --name myResourceGroup-dev --
location eastus
          az deployment group create \
            --resource-group myResourceGroup-dev \
            --template-file main.bicep \
            --parameters @parameters.dev.json

      - name: Deploy to staging
        if: github.ref == 'refs/heads/staging'
        run: |
          az group create --name myResourceGroup-staging
--location westus
          az deployment group create \
            --resource-group myResourceGroup-staging \
            --template-file main.bicep \
```

```
            --parameters @parameters.staging.json

      - name: Deploy to production
        if: github.ref == 'refs/heads/main'
        run: |
          az group create --name myResourceGroup-prod --
location centralus
          az deployment group create \
            --resource-group myResourceGroup-prod \
            --template-file main.bicep \
            --parameters @parameters.prod.json
        continue-on-error: true

      - name: Rollback production if deployment fails
        if: failure()
        run: |
          az deployment group create \
            --resource-group myResourceGroup-prod \
            --template-file main.bicep \
            --parameters @parameters.prod.rollback.json
```

In this workflow:

- The deployment steps deploy the Bicep template to the respective environment.

- The **continue-on-error** option allows the workflow to proceed to the rollback step even if the deployment fails.
- If the deployment to production fails, the workflow reverts to the previous stable configuration using **parameters.prod.rollback.json**.

Create Rollback Parameter File

Create a parameter file for the rollback configuration.

```
{
  "$schema":
"https://schema.management.azure.com/schemas/2019-04-
01/deploymentParameters.json#",
  "contentVersion": "1.0.0.0",
  "parameters": {
    "location": {
      "value": "centralus"
    },
    "storageAccountName": {
      "value": "previousprodstorageaccount"
    },
    "storageAccountType": {
      "value": "Standard_LRS"
    }
  }
}
```

Implementing Rollforward Strategy

For the rollforward strategy, I will fix the issue and deploy a new version. This approach requires maintaining versioned configurations and updating the deployment with the corrected configuration.

Setup GitHub Actions Workflow for Rollforward

I will modify the GitHub Actions workflow to include steps for deploying a corrected version.

```
name: Deploy Bicep Template


on:

  push:

    branches:

      - main

      - develop

      - staging


jobs:

  deploy:

    runs-on: ubuntu-latest


    steps:

      - name: Checkout repository

        uses: actions/checkout@v2
```

```
    - name: Set up Azure CLI
      uses: azure/cli@v1

    - name: Log in to Azure
      uses: azure/login@v1
      with:
        creds: ${{ secrets.AZURE_CREDENTIALS }}

    - name: Deploy to development
      if: github.ref == 'refs/heads/develop'
      run: |
        az group create --name myResourceGroup-dev --
location eastus
        az deployment group create \
          --resource-group myResourceGroup-dev \
          --template-file main.bicep \
          --parameters @parameters.dev.json

    - name: Deploy to staging
      if: github.ref == 'refs/heads/staging'
      run: |
        az group create --name myResourceGroup-staging
```

```
--location westus
          az deployment group create \
            --resource-group myResourceGroup-staging \
            --template-file main.bicep \
            --parameters @parameters.staging.json

      - name: Deploy to production
        if: github.ref == 'refs/heads/main'
        run: |
          az group create --name myResourceGroup-prod --
location centralus
          az deployment group create \
            --resource-group myResourceGroup-prod \
            --template-file main.bicep \
            --parameters @parameters.prod.json
        continue-on-error: true

      - name: Fix issue and deploy new version if
deployment fails
        if: failure()
        run: |
          echo "Fixing issue..."
```

```
        # Here you would include the steps to fix the
issue, e.g., updating parameters or template
        az deployment group create \
          --resource-group myResourceGroup-prod \
          --template-file main.bicep \
          --parameters @parameters.prod.fix.json
```

In this workflow:

- The deployment steps remain the same as before.
- The **continue-on-error** option allows the workflow to proceed to the fix step even if the deployment fails.
- If the deployment to production fails, the workflow includes steps to fix the issue and deploy a new version using **parameters.prod.fix.json**.

Create Fix Parameter File

Create a parameter file for the corrected configuration.

```
{
  "$schema":
"https://schema.management.azure.com/schemas/2019-04-
01/deploymentParameters.json#",
  "contentVersion": "1.0.0.0",
  "parameters": {
    "location": {
      "value": "centralus"
    },
    "storageAccountName": {
```

```
        "value": "newprodstorageaccount"
      },
      "storageAccountType": {
        "value": "Premium_LRS"
      }
    }
}
```

Testing the Strategies

To test both rollback and rollforward strategies, I can simulate deployment failures and observe how the workflows handle them.

Simulate a Failure and Test Rollback

```
# Create a failure in the main.bicep file to trigger rollback

echo "invalid syntax" >> main.bicep

git add main.bicep

git commit -m "Simulate failure to test rollback"

git push origin main
```

Simulate a Failure and Test Rollforward

```
# Fix the failure and test rollforward

git checkout main

echo "invalid syntax" >> main.bicep

git add main.bicep
```

```
git commit -m "Simulate failure to test rollforward"
git push origin main

# Fix the issue and update parameters.prod.fix.json
echo "Fixing issue..." >> main.bicep
git add main.bicep parameters.prod.fix.json
git commit -m "Fix issue and test rollforward"
git push origin main
```

Making use of rollback and rollforward strategies allows me to guarantee that my deployments are resilient and can bounce back fast from disappointments. By taking this route, I am able to strengthen my infrastructure's capacity to withstand deployment problems and resolve them efficiently.

Implementing Blue-Green Deployments

Deployment Stages

Blue-Green Deployment is a strategy that reduces downtime and risk by running two identical production environments: Blue and Green. Only one of these environments serves live production traffic at any given time. When a new version of the application is ready, it is deployed to the idle environment (e.g., Green). After thorough testing and verification, traffic is switched from the active environment (e.g., Blue) to the newly updated one (Green). If any issues are detected post-switch, traffic can be switched back to the previous environment (Blue), ensuring minimal downtime and seamless user experience.

Key steps in a Blue-Green Deployment include:

1. Deploy the new version of the application to the idle environment.
2. Perform tests to ensure the new environment is working correctly.
3. Redirect user traffic from the active environment to the new environment.
4. Monitor the new environment for any issues and validate that it is functioning as expected.

5. If issues are found, switch traffic back to the original environment.

Sample Program: Performing Blue-Green Deployment

My suggestion is that we use Azure's Blue-Green Deployment strategy to launch our project. In order to simulate the Blue and Green environments, we will use two sets of resources that are visually similar. Then, we will use Azure Traffic Manager to switch between the two sets of resources.

Setup Blue and Green Environments

First, I will create Bicep templates for the Blue and Green environments. These templates will deploy the same set of resources to different environments.

- Template File for Blue: **main.blue.bicep**

```
param location string = 'eastus'

param storageAccountName string = 'bluestorageaccount'

param storageAccountType string = 'Standard_LRS'


resource storageAccount
'Microsoft.Storage/storageAccounts@2019-04-01' = {

  name: storageAccountName

  location: location

  sku: {

    name: storageAccountType

  }

  kind: 'StorageV2'

  properties: {}

}
```

```
output storageAccountEndpoint string =
storageAccount.properties.primaryEndpoints.blob
```

- Template File for Green: **main.green.bicep**

```
param location string = 'westus'

param storageAccountName string = 'greenstorageaccount'

param storageAccountType string = 'Standard_LRS'


resource storageAccount
'Microsoft.Storage/storageAccounts@2019-04-01' = {

  name: storageAccountName

  location: location

  sku: {

    name: storageAccountType

  }

  kind: 'StorageV2'

  properties: {}

}


output storageAccountEndpoint string =
storageAccount.properties.primaryEndpoints.blob
```

Deploy Blue and Green Environments

Deploy the Blue and Green environments using Azure CLI or GitHub Actions.

- Deploy Blue Environment

```
# Create a resource group for the Blue environment

az group create --name myResourceGroup-blue --location
eastus


# Deploy the Blue environment

az deployment group create \

  --resource-group myResourceGroup-blue \

  --template-file main.blue.bicep
```

- Deploy Green Environment

```
# Create a resource group for the Green environment

az group create --name myResourceGroup-green --location
westus


# Deploy the Green environment

az deployment group create \

  --resource-group myResourceGroup-green \

  --template-file main.green.bicep
```

Setup Azure Traffic Manager

Azure Traffic Manager allows me to route user traffic between the Blue and Green environments. I will set up a Traffic Manager to manage the traffic switching.

- Create Traffic Manager Profile

```
# Create a Traffic Manager profile

az network traffic-manager profile create \

  --name myTrafficManagerProfile \

  --resource-group myResourceGroup-blue \

  --routing-method priority \

  --unique-dns-name myapp-trafficmanager \

  --ttl 30 \

  --protocol HTTP \

  --port 80
```

- Add Endpoints to Traffic Manager

Add the Blue and Green environments as endpoints to the Traffic Manager profile.

```
# Add Blue environment as the primary endpoint

az network traffic-manager endpoint create \

  --resource-group myResourceGroup-blue \

  --profile-name myTrafficManagerProfile \

  --name blueEndpoint \

  --type azureEndpoints \

  --target-resource-id $(az storage account show --name
bluestorageaccount --query id -o tsv) \

  --priority 1
```

```
# Add Green environment as the secondary endpoint

az network traffic-manager endpoint create \

  --resource-group myResourceGroup-green \

  --profile-name myTrafficManagerProfile \

  --name greenEndpoint \

  --type azureEndpoints \

  --target-resource-id $(az storage account show --name
greenstorageaccount --query id -o tsv) \

  --priority 2
```

Test and Switch Traffic

Initially, the Traffic Manager directs traffic to the Blue environment. After deploying a new version to the Green environment and verifying it, I can switch traffic to the Green environment.

- Switch Traffic to Green Environment

```
# Update the priority to switch traffic to the Green
environment

az network traffic-manager endpoint update \

  --resource-group myResourceGroup-green \

  --profile-name myTrafficManagerProfile \

  --name greenEndpoint \

  --priority 1


# Lower the priority of the Blue environment

az network traffic-manager endpoint update \
```

```
  --resource-group myResourceGroup-blue \
  --profile-name myTrafficManagerProfile \
  --name blueEndpoint \
  --priority 2
```

Monitor the Traffic Manager profile and the Green environment to ensure that it is handling traffic correctly. And, also validate the functionality and performance of the Green environment. If any issues are detected with the Green environment, switch back to the Blue environment by adjusting the priorities again.

- Switch Traffic Back to Blue Environment

```
# Update the priority to switch traffic back to the Blue environment
az network traffic-manager endpoint update \
  --resource-group myResourceGroup-blue \
  --profile-name myTrafficManagerProfile \
  --name blueEndpoint \
  --priority 1


# Lower the priority of the Green environment
az network traffic-manager endpoint update \
  --resource-group myResourceGroup-green \
  --profile-name myTrafficManagerProfile \
  --name greenEndpoint \
  --priority 2
```

The use of Blue-Green Deployments will allow me to minimize deployment-related downtime and associated risks. With this method, updating applications and infrastructure is a breeze, and you can test everything thoroughly and roll back quickly if needed.

Summary

So, we finally finished the last chapter of this book. I looked into different integration and deployment strategies for managing Bicep-based infrastructure deployments. I started by learning about the fundamentals of Continuous Integration and Continuous Deployment (CI/CD) and how these practices automate the process of integrating code changes and deploying them into production. I learned about Azure DevOps, a comprehensive suite of development tools that supports CI/CD pipelines, and how to configure pipelines with Bicep templates, GitHub Actions, and Azure DevOps.

I then looked into deploying to multiple environments, including development, staging, and production. I created environment-specific parameter files and set up GitHub Actions workflows to manage these deployments, ensuring consistency across multiple environments. This approach allowed me to thoroughly test changes in development and staging before putting them into production. Next, I learned rollback and rollforward strategies for dealing with deployment failures. I learned how to use a rollback strategy to return to a previous stable state and a rollforward strategy to deploy a corrected version to resolve issues. These strategies ensured that my deployments were resilient and could recover quickly after failures.

Finally, I learned Blue-Green Deployments, a method for reducing downtime and risk by running two identical production environments. I configured Blue and Green environments, used Azure Traffic Manager to route traffic between them, and learned how to monitor and validate deployments. This approach enabled me to update applications and infrastructure in a seamless manner, providing a robust mechanism to handle deployment issues while causing minimal disruption to users.

Overall, this chapter taught me advanced techniques for integrating Bicep into modern CI/CD pipelines, managing deployments across multiple environments, and implementing effective strategies to handle deployment failures, ensuring dependable and efficient infrastructure management.

Index

Epilogue

Coming to the conclusion of this book, I can't help but think back on the incredible adventure we've had. When I first started studying Azure Bicep, I was looking for a more efficient way to manage and deploy Azure assets. Through trial and error, countless hours of learning, and real-world application, I discovered Azure Bicep's true potential and how it can transform the way we approach infrastructure as code.

Writing "Azure Bicep QuickStart Pro" was an incredible experience. My goal was to create a resource that would help you, the reader, navigate the complexities of Azure Bicep, from the fundamentals to advanced deployment strategies. I hope that by sharing my experiences, challenges, and solutions, you have gained the knowledge and confidence to tackle your own projects with ease. Throughout this book, we've covered a variety of topics. We began with the fundamentals of JSON syntax and ARM templates, which laid a solid foundation for understanding Azure Bicep. We then looked at Bicep's declarative syntax, including parameters, conditions, and loops that enable dynamic and flexible deployments. We discussed the practical aspects of developing reusable modules, automating deployments with CI/CD pipelines, and managing multiple environments. I demonstrated how to handle deployment failures using rollback and rollforward strategies, as well as Blue-Green Deployments, which reduce downtime and risk during updates. Furthermore, we investigated secure parameter handling with Azure Key Vault to ensure that your deployments are both efficient and secure.

As you continue to work with Azure Bicep, I encourage you to experiment, learn, and push the limits of what is possible. The landscape of cloud computing and infrastructure as code is constantly changing, so remaining curious and adaptable is critical to success. Remember that the skills you learned from this book are only the beginning. Azure Bicep provides limitless options for optimizing and automating your infrastructure deployments. Whether you work on small projects or large-scale enterprise solutions, the principles and techniques you've learned here will be useful.

Thank you for selecting "Azure Bicep QuickStart Pro" as your guide. I hope this book has been a useful resource, enabling you to improve the efficiency and reliability of your Azure deployments. Your feedback and experiences are extremely valuable to me, so please share your thoughts and success stories. As we part ways, I wish you the best in your future endeavors. May your deployments run smoothly, your infrastructure be resilient, and your projects succeed. Continue exploring, innovating, and striving for excellence. Azure Bicep is a powerful tool that allows you to create amazing things.

Thank you, and happy deployment!

Kit Harrington

Thank You

www.ingramcontent.com/pod-product-compliance
Lightning Source LLC
Chambersburg PA
CBHW080211170726
48282CB00030B/1078
* 9 7 8 8 1 9 7 4 1 6 5 8 3 *